THE POLITICAL ECONOMY OF MARX

Oscar Luis Rigiroli

INDEX

ANALYTICAL INDEX

First Part

Prologue

Introduction

Chapter 1: Objectives and method of Marx.

Chapter 2 - Commodities

> Use value
>
> Exchange value
>
> Value and work
>
> Theory of fetishism

Chapter 3-Theory of value

> Value in the simple economy
>
> Value and price I
>
> Role of demand
>
> Limitations of the theory of labor value
>
> Role of the theory of value

Chapter 4 - Surplus value

> Analysis of the components of the value

FIRST PART

BASIC CONCEPTS

PROLOGUE

In writing this book I am among other things settling a debt with myself. Indeed, in my early teens in the early 1960s I militated for a brief period in a political movement in Buenos Aires, which in those days was a kind of Academy of Marxism, differentiated from both the official Communist Party, directly following the directives from Moscow in a time of Stalinism, and the Trotskyites groups, with voluntarist and more or less fanciful interpretations of reality. At the time, there was an implicit understanding in certain intellectual circles that the socialism of Marxist stamp would eventually prevail in the world, in view of the vigorous expansion it then enjoyed.

The meetings in which I participate had a theoretical rather than political or propaganda character, and included such readings and discussions on the Theory of Capitalist Development, by Paul Sweezy, of an unusual technical and intellectual density for those media.

I did not take too long to decide that Marxism was not my political position, but the seed of curiosity and interest in the study of Marxism was already planted in me, as well as the desire to deepen their basic applications and explore the deep reasons for my disagreement with some of its principles. Therefore this book began as a kind of political introspection, and was expanding its reach as I wrote it, in particular when I perceived that my research disclosed not so well known aspects of the writings of Marx.

At all times I have put objectivity in the analysis as a fundamental value, and hope to have succeeded to a large extent. My approach has been marked at all times by a deep respect for the subject and its actors, Kart Marx and his successors. I hope that it will be read as it tries to be: a contribution, by no means definitive, to divulge certain basic aspects of Marxist political economy, often overlooked by adherents and detractors. Therefore I put special emphasis in the discussion of certain early methodological choices made by Marx, that in my opinion have been crucial in the formulation of his economic analysis.

INTRODUCTION

"A ghost runs through Europe, the specter of communism," wrote Karl Marx and Friedrich Engels in the Communist Manifesto in 1848.

This ghost toured not only Europe but the world for roughly a century, as a promise or threat, and came to materialize in vast regions of the globe, dyed red, forming a block that looked compact and in continuous expansion for a long time. If we mentally go back to a time not so remote as 1950 for example, few well-informed and open minded people doubted that the planet future was Socialist or directly Communist. Although the two major conflicts in History, the two world wars, were not a the struggle between capitalism and communism, innumerable extremely bloody conflicts had it, and the axis of the world politics for decades was precisely the bid between the two blocks separated by the Iron Curtain.

The seduction exercised by socialism in its Marxist variant on the intellectuality of East and West was endearing and enduring, permeated and settled in all the social sciences, and to some extent extends even in our days, transformed into a dogma of a kind of secular religion.

Today the relentless tide of history has swept much of this two-faced promise, and this has happened in a relatively short period, of approximately one generation. To place an arbitrary milestone we will select the fall of the Berlin wall on the night of Thursday, November 9, 1989, for its symbolic value, but in fact the decline had begun well before.

The so feared nuclear conflagration between the two superpowers of the time, the United States of America and the Union of Soviet Socialist Republics, and their respective military and political blocs fortunately never took place, the anti-colonial revolts led by Communist guerrillas in Asia were mostly successful, ideological penetration in the West was intense, leading to the formation of Communist parties that were among the largest in their respective countries, and were aligned with the strategic needs of the USSR.

What happened? Why eclipse occurred in the influence of that ghost in such a short time? Investigating the political, military and strategic reasons for this global mutation is outside of the competence of this author and the purpose of this book. We rescue a central fact: economic competition between two systems, capitalist and communist, and prevalence of the first, unexpected for many people.

We will carry out our analyses starting from the basic tenets of communism as Karl Marx raised them, particularly in his book Capital, his summit work in the area of political economy and in reality a founding masterpiece of this branch of the economy.

As well as " the anatomy of civil society must be sought in political economy " according to the famous phrase of Marx in his contribution to the critique of political economy, the anatomy of Marxism should be sought in its own political economy. This means that the root of the successes and failures of Marxism must be traced to an appreciable extent to the formulations of the economic writings of Marx.

This book will intent to find the keys that guided the author from the methodological point of view in the adoption of his initial assumptions, determine what aspects that reality offered to him were taken and developed and of what other aspects he made abstraction. We will attempt to investigate whether the conclusions obtained by Marx and his theories and predictions about the future of capitalism are a direct and rational consequence of those original options. Finally, we will explore how time treated these theories and particularly the predictions.

To perform this task we will be discussing in detail each of the major themes of Marxism, unfolding its meaning and putting it in the context of the other concepts. Finally, in each issue, we will do a critique of the its content and will seek to clarify what functioned well over time and what failed.

We will do this analysis with due respect to the author, taking into account that wrote in a relatively early stage of the globalization of capitalism, although perhaps he himself was not aware of that, while we have at least three key pieces of information that Marx did not have:

• The fact that capitalism has survived a century and a half, and presently shows enjoying of all its forces, which surely wasn't expected to Marx.

• The experience of real socialism over more than seven decades, and which still continues to some extent; in that period the possibilities latent in the Marxist formulation were explored by many of the best brains in every age. The indisputable fact is that the theory of Marx had all opportunities to prove itself.

• Checking, also experimental, of capitalism, even without changing its basic features.

He managed to incorporate huge reforms, perhaps not readily, which improved the luck and the living conditions of huge masses of population, still retaining its character of employees, so are the problem today not the workers but the sectors that have failed to join the system.

- The experimental verification that capitalism, even without changing its basic characteristics, incorporated huge reforms, perhaps not willingly, which improved luck and living conditions of vast masses of the population, while retaining their character of employees, so that the problem is not today the situation of workers but the ample sectors that have failed to join the system.

The writer has attempted to write this book in simple language, with common use words and without jargon, not to insiders but to interested parties. Cumbersome lengthy direct quotes from Capital or other texts written by Marx, usually dense and sometimes of slow understanding, which are common in other authors who treated his work, have been overlooked here, for the benefit of the expression of the central concepts directly.

Algebraic derivations, common in the works of Marx, have been used, but in each case the non familiar reader is alerted that he can skip them until the conclusions are reached without losing its meaning. Deep mathematical or economy knowledge are definitely not needed for reading this book, just a good dose of intellectual curiosity and open-mindedness.

We hope that this route will enable us to learn more about the thought of Marx, as full of luminous analysis as of unfulfilled prophecies.

CHAPTER 1

Objectives and methods of Marx

Marx started studying what he called political economy after a long process during which he was defining his sphere of interests. Understanding the basic features of this process is essential to grasp the reasons for certain choices made at the beginning of his analysis which decisively shaped his interpretation of social phenomena. The central objective of Marx was revealing the economic law of motion of modern society.

That goal, and the choices made eventually would lead him to assert that the "anatomy of civil society should be sought in the political economy", luminoussentence, particularly at his relatively early time of social research. It follows that it is not sporadic changes in the self-consciousness of human beings that cause movements in society but, on the contrary, changes in social existence, which are determined by what he called "modes of production, are then reflected in the legal and political aspects. To put it in Marxist terminology, changes in the productive infrastructure determine movements in the legal, moral and even religious superstructure of societies.

This finding would lead him to manifest that the engine of social change is the mutation in the mode of production. This is simply a logical conclusion based on the above premise: changes in the way in which the society produces decisively transform their anatomy, to follow the biological metaphor.

Now the next logical question is: what is the nature of this change in the mode of production, which has the potential to transform the entire legal and political superstructure? In principle, the answer is not obvious. The changes in the mode of production can be of a technological nature, be based on access to new sources of production factors: raw materials, labor, energy, etc. Marx makes automatically an election that would be central in the course of his ulterior work. He was under the powerful intellectual influence of Hegel's philosophy, in particular the dialectic method that describes the processes and developments as a result of the conflict between opposing and contradictory forces. The method that sees in the antagonism between two opposite principles, thesis and antithesis, and in its resolution in a synthesis the natural course of development of all kinds of processes, including social is well known. The use of dialectic leads Marx to choose a specific source of conflict: the struggle of classes. Marx traces in the great historical changes an underlying class conflict, of which he studied in depth the struggles between nobles and burghers in the advent of capitalism.

At times in history, the development of the material forces of production (including here those of technological origin, new inputs, etc.) conflict with what Marx calls "production relations" basically property relations, particularly the property of production means. These property relations act as a brake that stops the economic development until the pressure change dynamites the whole superstructure and replaces it by a new set of property relations more functional to new developments.

In this way, the sequence of events in the revolutionary periods would be as follows:

Changes in the material base of production make that relations of production, that is relations of property, constitute a corset that prevents the economic development. This exacerbates conflicts of class based on the relations of property in force, until the dialectical conflict is overcome through a new synthesis, i.e. new property relations.

Marx used the method of what we would call today successive approximations, making abstraction - i.e. removing temporarily- all the elements that are not decisive for the stage of analysis in which he was interested at that moment. In this way he could lay bare the anatomy of the problem, and reintroduce the eliminated items when analyzing the issue in stages of a lesser level of abstraction. The assumption underlying this method is that the elimination of issues leading to high degrees of abstraction will be so that general conclusions extracted at such a high level will continue to be valid when it drops to a degree lower than abstraction, i.e. when previously eliminated elements are reintroduced. In other words, the high degree of abstraction should eliminate secondary or superfluous details so as to be able to view the essential structure of the problem under study, but when returning to more specific levels the obtained structure should remain valid. Otherwise, what had been cleared at the start were essential elements that should not have been abstracted. We will see later how some analyses of Marx perform in this aspect.

CHAPTER 2

Commodities

The first chapter of Capital is dedicated to commodities. The clear definition and consistent use of this concept is central in all the work of Marx. Commodity is any product that is made for exchange and not to the use of the producer. Therefore, the notion of commodity is from its conception tied to the exchange.

As well as many economists before and after, Marx began studying the simplest case, called the simple production of commodities. In this case, a given producer, working for himself - not for an employer - and using his own tools and equipment, produces a type of commodity in quantities greater than that those necessary for his use, and covers his needs (and obviously those of his family) of the more diverse commodities through the exchange of their surplus production with other producers, that act in the same way. There is no more basic form of exchange than this, and it allows us to clearly study the characteristics of this social fact.

In the case of the economy of barter, a commodity which we will call M1 is exchanged by the producer 1 by another commodity M2 that he requires to meet his needs; the circuit of barter is thus M-M, without any instance interposed between the two commodities. In this case, the producer 1 should look to other producers 2, 3 etc. who need what he produces, and inversely who produce what he needs. When money appears, in any of the physical manifestations which had been used for transactions in history (cattle, shells, accounts, coins, banknotes, and the current more abstract forms of money) transactions are divided into two parts: our producer 1 changes his product M1 by an amount of money D, the first transaction will then be described as M1-D, and then with D he leaves to search for suppliers of other commodities necessary for their use, for example M2, making the transaction D-M2. The great advantage is that no longer the producer 2, who offers product 2, simultaneously requires the product 1. This facilitates and lubricates all economic transactions with respect to the simple barter system and had long before the advent of capitalism, a great importance in the development of human societies.

Other economists such as Adam Smith had already directed their attention to exchange, linking it to the concept of division of labor. Schematically, we will establish that the division of labor allows the growth of productivity, maximizing the amount of assets available to a society, and that exchange closes the loop by allowing each producer to dispose of their surpluses and to meet their own needs. Division of labor and exchange are two facts necessarily related, and one explains each other. Marxists criticize the conception of Smith on the grounds that he does not conceive work division separately from exchange, and therefore links the former necessarily to the concept of commodity, which would become a category derived from the nature of mankind and inescapable. Marx retains the leading role of the division of labor, but reduced commodities to a historical category, which appears in a certain phase of human evolution and is likely to disappear in the future. While recognizing that the production of commodities is very old, he states that there have been certain civilizations where the division of labor was not linked to the exchange of commodities, but the products of the different types of work were shared by social, usually small and primitive groups. In other words, the production of commodities is for Marx not the exclusive and compulsory form of economic activity. What obviously interested him was not so much analyze the division of labor in the past, but prove that it would be possible in the future even though the concept of commodity were replaced.

Although it is said implicitly in the above, it should be highlighted that the production of commodities is not exclusive of the capitalist system but prior to its existence, and that the advent of the same was only possible once commodity production had reached a level of significant development. What is characteristic of this system is that the manufacture of commodities is the almost exclusive form of production, relegating other historical categories (related to various forms of servitude) to almost extinction.

Marx was interested in discovering the social relations hidden behind commodities and exchange. Indeed, behind the relationship between products (quantitative relationships based on their prices), he wanted to put in evidence the relations between producers, social relations based on qualitative facts.

This choice of Marx is consistent with what is already expressed in the previous chapter, and the successive options which will take place later. What counts in the economic facts are relationships between producers, i.e., among individuals who occupy determined roles in the framework of production and exchange. Other factors affecting the production of commodities fall outside his focus of attention. Usually the major elections have consequences, and without a doubt this is no exception. We are studying the simple production of commodities and is still very early to determine if placing the social relations of production almost as the sole determinant is leaving out essential elements study to explain socio-economic change, such as technological factors, availability of resources, etc.

As we are human, we find placing relationships between people in the centre attractive and natural, but we cannot exclude that other essential forces are dimmed by this decision. We will return to this topic ahead.

For subsequent analyses, Marx makes a fundamental distinction between use value and exchange value of commodities. We will see both concepts with some detail.

Use value

This concept expresses the utility that the commodity provides the user, and for that reason Marx called it alternately utility. Ultimately it makes reference to the need of the user that the good satisfies. It follows that the value in use is a relationship between the consumer and the consumed object, and not a relationship between different users or producers, i.e. a social relationship. As Marx has restricted the scope of the economy to social relationships, i.e. relationships between people, use value falls outside the scope of his definition of political economy.

This is not the only possible definition. Indeed many economists define economics as the set of relationships between individuals and commodities, so the value of use or usefulness plays an essential role in their respective areas of study.

Exchange value

Marx called the exchange value simply value. While the value of exchange appears at first sight as a quantitative relationship between objects, behind this appearance Marx reveals a relationship between the producers of those objects, i.e., a relationship between individuals, a social relation, and therefore, faithful to his definitions seen before, made the exchange value an essential political economy category. Although, within the model of simple commodity production, the producers seem to be working independent and isolated from each other, exchange reveals that they are actually working for one another. Ultimately, the exchange value shows that commodities are products of human work in a society based on the division of labor, in which producers carry out their tasks in a private and independent way. At the risk of being repetitive, we will emphasize once again that the commodities and their value of exchange are a trait of a type of society based on the following characteristics: division of labor and private production.

Value and work

The requirement imposed by Marx to be expressions of social relations economic categories leads naturally to the question of what is the source or origin of the exchange value: in a simple commodity production society such source cannot be other than human work, which is "the value that lies hidden behind the exchange value".

Human labor is the expenditure of brain, nerves and muscles that lead to the production of commodities, to be devoted to exchange, and conversely, the work products are materialized human activity.

As well as Marx distinguishes between two types of value- the use value or usefulness, and the exchange value or simply value- he discerns also two types of work. One is what he calls "useful work", which is what develops a weaver, a carpenter, a blacksmith, etc. , and give as products commodities that meet certain needs, creating use values. Then, useful work is the source of value in use, and like that one, falls outside the scope of study of the economy according to Marx.

On the other hand, the exchange value of a commodity, or value, is created by the expenditure of human labor in general, nonspecific, which he called "abstract labor", and which is the consumption of labor power of producers. This abstract work is thus the source of the exchange value of commodities, and is a subject of study in the Marxist political economy. To sum up this point, Marx can say that the source of the value (of exchange) is the (abstract) work.

Also in this case, since we are human beings, this expression is attractive since it links the notion of value exclusively to our activity. We should however remember that the reasoning which has led to formulate it is one the set out, and that is based on strict definitions of Marx which can be shared or not by other scholars.

The concept of abstract labor is not an original contribution of Marx. As he himself warns us, it is present with different names in classical economists such as Benjamin Franklin, Adam Smith and David Ricardo, and the differences between these concepts are actually of detail. It is not an abstract work in the sense of metaphysical or mysterious, but in the sense of generic working, not related to a specific or particular activity. Capitalist society has made permeable to a large extent the boundaries between professions and trades, which are crossed by large contingents of workers migrating from obsolete jobs to other more updated, through a certain job retraining. Therefore, the crucial point for a society at a given time is not how many workers there are in one or the other branch of activity considered as watertight compartments, but the total labor force and their qualitative degree of development. This does not deny that labor mobility from one post to another and from one region to another is not always painless, but if means that in capitalism a worker whose job has become obsolete is not necessarily doomed to poverty and inactivity, but can return to other areas of production, a level unattainable in the past.

Theory of fetishism

The fetishism theory plays a central role in the political economy of Marx.

In the capitalist economy, marked by the production of commodities, producers rarely come into contact with each other, and the social nature of the process is made clear in the act of exchanging. Each producer meets with the users of the product of his work through the market, where quantities and prices of exchanged commodities are agreed. What should be a social relationship between producers - argues Marx - assumes the "fantastic" form of the relationship between things-including money- in the eyes of men. The social relationship is "reified". Commodities are separated from their producers and stand in front to them by imposing their own rules of change; ultimately things dominate their creators.

In past times, according to Marxist thought, change relationships had a personal character: a potter physically met and traded his vessels with a weaver who in turn provided him with his fabrics, and a hunter changed his hares with a basket producer. There was objectification and the social nature of the relationship was put in evidence. There was no market standing between the producers and issuing them with its rules.

What can we think of this last statement? Except in the case of a hunter and a weaver who lived alone in their world, separated from all other human community (in which example is doubtful that we could speak of a "social" relationship), the producers who met personally did not do it in a vacuum. A series of exchanges preceding them, and certain parameters were taken into account when changing hares by baskets. Marx himself dedicated much effort to this topic to develop his theory of work value. I.e., within the frame of exchanges there were elements that preexisted the meeting between producers and set them certain values of reference, in particular the relationship between the efforts required to achieve one product and the other, as it will propose definitive Marx. The rudiments of the concepts that eventually would crystallize in markets already existed and were external to the producers who came to negotiate.

What is the reason that Marx assigns so much importance to this topic? When terms of trade are reified and the so called "factors of production" (land, labor, capital) are placed outside their possessors and opposite to them, defenders of the current system attributed to each of these factors the property of generating income for their owners who negotiate the distribution of the income among wages, benefits, rent and interest. Thus, economic agents come together in relationships that end up erecting a vast ethical and legal superstructure, appearing as it is a negotiation between equals, each with eligibility for a category of income (wages, profit, etc). This darkens, in Marxist thought, the true reality of exploitation that underlies the essence of capitalism and gives it an acceptable varnish. What happens is that the ultimate purpose of Marxist political economics is that of stripping the underlying conflicts of class in the production of commodities, form in which the production of goods is expressed in capitalism. Therefore Marx seeks to highlight that the mentioned economic relations and the superstructure are not a natural and necessary feature of every time and place, but only the one they acquire at a historical stage dominated by capitalism.

Returning to the theory of fetishism, it remains the question if the relationships between people and other factors of production are only an appearance, a ghost, a fetish, as Marx argues, and if the only real relationships are those which exist between the producers. This is equivalent to removing from the study of economics the objective relationships between different economic categories (people and things).

In History, despite the similarity between the processes occurring in different places, the availability of resources and technological advances has strongly conditioned the degree of development of the respective societies. The status of relations between producers and things does not affect its social character.

It is one thing to give priority to the relations between producers to elucidate the characteristics of certain relations, abstracting temporarily from that level the relations with things (products, markets, price levels) with the implicit commitment to reintroduce them at a lower abstraction level, and another thing is to attribute to such elements an unreal and fantastic character.

CHAPTER 3

Theory of value

The problem of the quantitative value or value, creation of Marx theory although based on some pre-existing ideas, plays a central role in the construction of his political economy.

Marx begins with a clear premise: at all times there is a total workforce in a society. Each historical type of society distributes that labor mass in particular branches of production according to laws that are specific to that type of society, and which ultimately depend on other broader laws operating in that particular society. But, emphasizes the author, there is always a law presiding over this distribution, it is not an arbitrary or random process.

In a company producing commodities, particularly in the capitalist society, the exchange value of the former is the essential aspect that governs the allocation of productive resources between the various branches, and the theory of value is the key to carrying out such distribution.

Our author departs of two obvious observations: each type of commodity absorbs a portion of the total workforce of the society, and they are exchanged in the market according to certain proportions that are relatively stable and do not seem arbitrary. Now, which is the relationship between both facts: absorption of a portion of the total workforce and exchange relationship?

Marx presupposes that there is a correlation between working time dedicated to produce specific commodities and their exchange value. It is not a generic relationship or a certain loose linking both values, but a direct proportionality (with certain particulars that we will deal with afterwards). Here it can be inferred that the source of the exchange value or simply value is the content of work of a particular good, measured in units of time. Ultimately, the value of a commodity depends on the strength of work necessary for its production,

At this point it becomes necessary to add a precision on the workforce concept. It is also a commodity, and therefore corresponds to calculate its value using the general law: the value of the labor force is determined by the time required to generate that commodity, in this case the time required to produce the subsistence commodities necessary for maintaining and reproducing the worker and his family.

How would the creator of political economy face the obvious productivity differences that exist between different individuals, originating in their training and labor skills, in their attitude towards work, his industriousness or laziness, his intelligence or other individual factors? Logically a commodity produced by a lazy or low-skilled worker will not have a greater market value than one made by a skilled and highly qualified workman, simply by the fact that the first it takes longer in producing it, or more time consuming work: Marx solves this problem by clarifying that what really counts is not the working time of one single worker or other, but the significant one is what calls the "socially necessary time" for the production of the commodity. In every social environment there is a time that is needed to produce a given good having in account the usual equipment, expertise and contraction to work that are usual in that society, a sort of average time.

How to face the challenge presented to the theory the time spent by a highly skilled worker? Our author meets it arguing that qualified labor is equivalent to the simple socially necessary work, but intensified, or multiplied by a given factor; i.e. a qualified working time unit is equivalent to more than one single working unit.

How can the equivalence between the unit of qualified work and simple work be calculated? Obviously the relationship between the values created by one and another cannot be taken as a basis, because this would lead to the following circular reasoning: the qualified job creates more value than the simple work, and this is so because the created value is greater.

Aside from differential skills from one worker to another, already observed in by the average character of the socially necessary work, Marx explains the intensification of qualified work produced by the training received previously. To quantify the productivity of both workers, the skilled and the simple worker, he sets a ratio between the labor life in the qualified worker hours, and the time in hours of the required training, including his own time of learning and that of his coaches. If that socially necessary training time is equivalent, say 50% of the workers useful life, each time unit of qualified labor will be equivalent to 1, 5 units of simple work.

This simple accounting with which Marx believed to have resolved the differences in productivity among workers, that could hardly be ignored in assessing the value created by them (whatever be the interpretation of the word value, topic on which we will return) presented problematic facets whose impact have increased over time. We will return to this later.

Value in simple Economy

Nothing better to illustrate the functioning of this concept in a market of simple or primitive economy than the well known example (used by Marx) of the negotiation of commodities exchange between a deer hunter and a beaver hunter. If a beaver hunt takes twice as long as that of a deer, the only possibility to swap them in an equitable manner is precisely in that proportion, two deer by a beaver. If they changed in another proportion, for example one to one, nobody would hunt beavers and all would go hunting deer. But on the other hand a new factor comes into play: If beavers are hunted only for making hats, while the deer is the staple food of hunting people, it is logical that the need to hunt the latter will be much greater than that of the first. So beside the supply factors appear the demand ones. As we will see later in this chapter. Marx, unlike contemporary economists did not devote much space to studies of demand. We must note that we find in this example, not only pre-capitalist but pre-agricultural, the elements that define exchange in a bourgeois society: production for exchange based on the division of labor, the existence of a rudiment of market, and a mechanism for the determination of the value of the commodities that are applicable to capitalism. This is not opposed in any way with the teachings of our thinker, who emphasized that the characteristic and differentiation of capitalism is that the production of commodities is virtually the exclusive way that unfolds in such a system.

Value and price I

We have seen that in the Marxist terminology value is synonymous with exchange value, or the ratio in which the goods are exchanged to each other. But it is not a magnitude that can readily replace the price of commodities, which as we know has many components, many of them extremely volatile. Indeed in addition to its content of manpower real prices are determined by a constellation of factors including their scarcity or relative abundance at the time of the transaction, content of various raw materials, novelty, existence and prices of substitutes, seasonal factors, macroeconomic reasons and a long etcetera. All this produces a greater or lesser variability of prices, sometimes within short time intervals. In practice, there is an inability to use value in the Marxist sense instead of the price concept.

In order to reach a settlement between the two concepts, Marx argues that the value is the amount that the price of a commodity must converge in circumstances of balance of the quantities offered and demanded. In his own words: "at the time in which the supply and demand are balanced, and therefore fail to act, the market price of a commodity will match its value". It is suggestive that Marx made by one of its rare mentions of the demand in this context.

Role of demand

Indeed, demand and wishes of the consumer never formed part of Marxist political economics, and this negligence has had an impact in the non-conformity of the populations with the shortage of goods characteristic of the collectivist societies, and the citizens dissatisfaction by this circumstance was undoubtedly an ingredient in the fall of the USSR and the Soviet bloc as a whole.

The reasons for the Marxist contempt for the role of demand and ultimately for the consumer derives from two converging reasons.

On the one hand the fact that class differences exert a role on demand, by limiting the expenditures that the proletariat can perform. This leads to presume (with full justification at the time and still today largely) that demand of the working class is reduced to those absolutely indispensable subsistence commodities. This is rather obvious and does not justify an extensive theoretical treatment.

Indeed, for the proletariat, and for society as a whole, the reality is that resources are always insufficient to cope with endless needs. This however was not an obstacle for other schools of economic thought developed in-depth studies on demand and the role of consumers, which gave importance to the satisfaction of the needs of these, what is highlighted in current consumer societies.

The other reason why Marx scorned the role of consumers is that according to his own expression he was looking for "the economic law of motion of modern society", i.e. the engines of change, and attributed to demand a reactive character, not dynamic or determinant of such change, believing that profound mutations can only happen triggered of other factors. Hardly can this conclusion be shared now, taking into account the dizzying changes in the demanded products, the success of certain commodities and the failure of others, world's wide divergences in demand for commodities, and even within a given society, the differences for example of different age groups. Changes in demand have caused mutations of the supply of commodities of great magnitude, and its purely reactive character is called into question because of the difficulty in predicting which products will be successful and which will fail. Although such analysis belongs to a lower level of abstraction in which Marx was moving, a demand analysis is an essential feature in an economic theory. It was not included in his priorities simply because it did not conform to his central scheme and his predetermined objective.

Limitations of the theory of labor value

There are several considerations that limit the application of the theory of value in practice. This happens when we descend on the level of abstraction in the direction of a greater approximation to reality. We will see some of them:

1. We said that in situations of balance between supply and demand, actual prices tend to values. A first problem with this interpretation is the same concept of balance. Marx himself spends a good deal of his work (which we will see in chapters especially dedicated to them) to the crisis of the capitalist system, and predicted that they would be more frequent and stronger, that they would jeopardize the stability of the system and eventually cause his downfall. These crises are basically more or less violent apartments of economic

equilibriums. Both in the mentioned Marx studies as well as in subsequent works of economists from other schools, including Schumpeter, it becomes clear that constant imbalances and large fluctuations are not a marginal but undesirable characteristic of the capitalist system, but their normal means of self-purging and growth (see some paragraphs dedicated to the interpretation of Schumpeter in the chapters dedicated to the crisis). Of course, Governments try to avoid the most devastating consequences of such crises and fluctuations through anti cyclic policies in order to preserve the populations of extreme pain and preserve their own stability as Governments. In any case, the fact that the mutations and imbalances are a constant in the economic system is undeniable. This translates into the everyday experience that prices vary constantly, and they do it in a way that is clearly not based on the time of work necessary for the production of commodities. In reality employers make their decisions of prices not according to their values of working time, but according to their overall cost structure. In these structures the cost of labor (clarify: not its value, but its price) is one of the factors together with raw materials, auxiliary materials, the costs of energy and infrastructure, depreciation, interest, taxes and other inputs. Assuming that each of those factors moves in turn around their respective values lacks realism....

2. In reality what Marx had in view in his time was a labor universe in which the proportion of skilled workers was small, and in which the rating difference between the

specialized and simple workers was relatively small. In this context, in reality the author could make use of abstraction (as we saw in Chapter 1 when we treat the methodological aspects) and ignore the extent of those differences in productivity, assigning them a relatively minor importance. This is arguably true today, when the differences in productivity between different workers are enormous, according to their profession, equipment, training, geographic location, productive branch and context in which work, organizational issues, etc., and cannot be compensated by the algorithm proposed on the basis of the ratio between working life and social time invested in their training, which today looks clearly insufficient.

3. In the 19th century, the idea that the decisive factor of the "value" was the content of work or labor force was self-evident. The industries were mainly manufacturing, and in the process industries such as steel or textile, the contingents of workers were very numerous and involved in many stages of production. With mechanization, automation, computerization and robotics in the industrial and economic processes in general, this has changed decisively and the incidence of the role of the workforce is no longer so evident.

Role of the theory of value

In a system based on the production of commodities, as the capitalist society, the value of commodities regulates the forces that determine: i) rates to commodities are exchanged between them, ii) the quantities of each commodity produced and iii) the distribution of labor between different branches of production. Marx's work-value theory tries to explain on the basis of which parameters capitalism comes to resolve the points (i) to (iii), taking into account that there is no authority that set those values.

The abstract determination of what constitutes the value of a good is somewhat subjective, and there have been various theories of value in history, according to the circumstances in which economic activity unfolded, and in each case the answer seemed intuitively correct; for example: in the mercantilist stage it was conceived that the value was determined by the relationship between the utility of the good and its shortage, which resulted in precisely the scarcity theory. In the explosion of the manufacturing stage comes the theory of value of Marx (in fact with a background in classical economists), and if someone imposed is today unlikely mission to formulate a theory of value, it is likely to make at least some reference to contents of know-how or scientific and technological knowledge in the commodity in question. In short, the practical use of a theory of value is relative, since as we have seen, does not ensure that the commodities will be exchanged effectively with reference to its precepts.

CHAPTER 4

Surplus value

We have commented above that capitalism is not the only society where the production of commodities, based on the division of labor and exchange has taken place. We will now see one of the distinctive features that separate capitalism from other earlier forms of organization with commodities production.

In the simple commodity production we have seen two different producers, each working with its working tools and other means of production (land, buildings, facilities, animals charge, etc.) that found on the marketplace and exchange their products to meet their needs and those of their families.

In the capitalist economy the means of production are held by a small group of agents - the capitalists - while the work is carried out by another group. The difference with the simple production is that one of the main exchanges does not occur between two owners of means of production, but between a group of holders of the same, and another group that only has its members' workforce to sell. It is important to emphasize that what workers sell is not their work but their labor force, i.e. the ability to perform work, which is sold to the capitalist making available to him their time during a certain number of hours to carry out the tasks entrusted to them. The buying and selling of labor force is, therefore, the essential feature of capitalism.

We reiterate that in the simple production the reason that leads to the individual producer to market is obtaining by exchange the goods that he is missing; then he enters the market with goods (M1) and comes with goods (M2), certainly different from those that led to sell. The circuit is therefore in this case M1-M2

Different is the case of the capitalist who enters the circuit of exchange of commodities. Originally he has an amount of money (symbolized with D1), which he spends buying commodities that are present in the market, including raw materials and materials, labor force, and if newly installed, machinery, buildings and installations. We call M the set of these commodities. Finally, after the process of industrialization, if any, he sells his products to exchange them again for an amount of money D2. Logically this D2 amount must be greater than D1 so the entire process makes sense, and the entrepreneur has a motivation for his actions. The circuit that the capitalist runs through in the act of production is thus:

$$D1-M-D2$$

So while in the case of simple commodity production the difference between the commodities with which each producer enters and leaves the exchange is qualitative, in the case of the capitalist, the difference between the amounts D in input and output is quantitative.

The question formulated by Marx is what the source from which it comes the creation of value - called surplus value by him - that is kept by the entrepreneur, since reasonably, he argues, that may not have emerged from nowhere. Then he analyzes the various factors of production, to determine which of them can be that source. He discards the means of production, which, he argues, increase the amount of produced commodities transferring them part of its own value: the total value in the case of raw materials and materials, and part of its value in the case of machinery, installations and buildings (which today would depreciation and amortization). But the amount transferred to the products is deducted from the value of the means of production, which are consumed in the process; in this way there is no net creation of value, only transfer. Therefore it ruled out as the source of value creation.

He also discarded liquid or financial capital, to which does not assign any ability to create value, looking at it as sterile from that point of view.

The only possibility left is work, to which Marx assigns the power to generate all of the new value created in the production process.

On the intimate detail of the creation of value by the worker, Marx argues in the following manner: the capitalist has acquired a day of the worker, which has agreed to pay him a sum in exchange for, say twelve hours of work. At the end of a fraction of that time such as six hours, the worker has created value by the same amount that the employer will pay to him. If production stopped at that moment, the capitalist would have not increased his assets, only would have compensated the amount paid to his employee, and there would be no surplus value. But in fact the worker will continue working for another six hours (in the example of Marx), and what he produces in this second period is what increases the richness of his employer, and is ultimately the source of all value. The surplus value is thus that value created by the worker and not paid to him.

According to this analysis, the total working time is divided into two parts: the time required to meet the vital needs of the worker and his family, and the time to create surplus value.

The specificity of capitalism is not, according to our author, the exploitation of workers but exploitation through the creation of surplus value.As with all the important concepts of Marxism, we will stop a few moments to reflect on the definition of surplus value.

The entire political economy of Marx is aimed to highlight the relationship of subordination between capital and labor. All his choices and definitions are oriented in this direction, and the surplus value plays a central role in that framework. The key decision is to whom he assigns the character of responsible for the creation of value. If, as Marx argues, only work is bearer of the ability to create value, the fact that the capitalist appropriates at the end of the cycle of a portion of that value (surplus value), necessarily implies that he took from its creator, the worker. This implies that the origin of the business profit is spoliation. As we said, this reflection of Marx is consistent with his previous and subsequent elections. But not all are happy with this exclusive character in the creation of value. Other economists argue that without the participation of the capitalist, which is who possesses, brings together and organizes the factors of production, including work, land and buildings, machinery and facilities, raw materials and materials and leadership, work alone could not pass beyond of the stadium of simple production of commodities, which we saw at the beginning. Thus- in this view- the own capitalist is the source of that surplus value, and he has not taken it away from anyone. Without wishing to take part in a war of definitions more or less arbitrary and subjective, it may be agreed in general that is just the spatial and temporal convergence of all factors enunciated before- including in particular labor and the organizing element, whether of private or public character- which enables the production of that excedent that we will continue calling surplus value.

It is necessary also to highlight the social importance of the existence of surplus value. Aside from covering the expenses of private capitalists, through the mechanism of productive investment it is the source of the creation of new industries, the expansion of the existing ones to meet the demand of a growing population with permanent new needs, and the generation of new jobs; also is the source of taxes collection that redistributes wealth providing (unfortunately not always) services of health, education, security, infrastructure, etc. to always more complex communities. The prolonged existence of socialist economies for more than seven decades did not involve the disappearance or decrease of the surplus value, only its appropriation and not always for the benefit of workers.

Analysis of the components of value

Marx finds three distinguishable components within the value of a commodity. In the foreground are the elements that "do not undergo a change in their quantitative value during the production process" and that are why they are called **constant capital** and denoted with the letter **c.** This part of the capital is represented by raw materials, auxiliary materials (packaging, etc.) and the machines and facilities used in the production process, which do not undergo changes in their value in the sense that it is incorporated into the good produced. The second part, usually called **variable capital** and symbolized by the letter **v** undergoes changes throughout the production cycle, as it not only replenishes its own value but also produces, as we have seen, an excedent. The third part is precisely this **surplus value** produced by human work, and designated with **s**. The total value of commodities **w** is then the sum of three components:

$$w = c + v + s$$

This formula and its components go beyond the value of an isolated commodity, and it can be used to analyze the production of a company, industry or country during a certain period, e.g. one year.

Making a comparison with modern economic concepts more familiar to many readers, **w** denotes the production of a commodity or industry at wholesale prices, **c** is the consumption of raw materials and depreciation of equipment, **v** represents payments of wages and other remuneration, and **s** benefits, rent and interests paid to the owners of capital. The value added by a company or industry branch is the sum of **v+ s** plus that part of **c** corresponding to the depreciation of equipment. The concept of a country's GDP (gross domestic product) corresponds to the same definition.

In accounting terms, the part of **c** corresponding to raw materials and auxiliary materials are part of the working capital, while the part of **c** which represents machinery and facilities constitutes fixed capital put into play in the production process. It should be added that only that part of these machines and installations that are consumed in each business cycle (i.e. what we consider accounting depreciation) form part of the **c** considered in the formation of **w**.

The formula **w= c+v+s** plays an important role in Marxist political economy. Marx defines several ratios among its terms, and gives those ratios proper names, in order to develop his analysis. We will see these definitions in the next points

Surplus value rate

The surplus value or exploitation rate **s´** is the quotient of surplus value **s** and variable capital **v**, according to the expression:

$$s'= s/v$$

The dividend and the divisor of this ratio can be given in units of time (hours of work) or in cash (assigning a value to each hour of work, paid or not), but in both cases **s'** will be a dimensionless number (without units) and may be expressed as a percentage. For example, in the previous case in that the worker worked 12 hours a day, and the necessary time to obtain his subsistence means was 6 hours, the value of the rate of surplus value will be:

s'= 6 hs / 6hs= 1, i.e. a rate of surplus value of 100

Ultimately the rate of surplus value indicates how many hours does the employee work for his employer per each hour he works for himself, i.e. to sustain himself and his family.

The value of the rate of surplus value can be increased by the capitalist (which logically is his objective) basically in three ways:

• Prolonging the duration of the working day and keeping fixed the "required hours of work" (to sustain the worker, i.e. the hours which he pays the worker).

• Decreasing the required hours of work, the part of the day that is paid to the worker, which means lower wages.

• Increasing worker productivity, for example through more and better production means (machinery, methods, etc, which ultimately also produces a decline in the required hours of work in relation to the total, but not in a loss of wages.

Obviously, moves in these variables in the opposite direction will mean a decline in the surplus value rate, which will not occur by the will of the employer, but may happen for example by the entry into force of new labor laws that limit the length of the working day or increase wages or others factors of different origin that decrease the productivity (e.g. lack of power or for technical failures are out of service equipment).

Marx assumes that the rate of surplus value in a society and at a given moment is homogeneous in the various branches of production, despite being aware that this is not strictly true. However, he reasons, there are forces in the interior of that society which tend to standardize it, for example the migration of labor force from one branch to another in search less exploitation, and the divestment of the capital of certain branches and its reinvestment in others of higher rate of surplus value.

We will again ask us about the reality of this forced homogenization of the rates of surplus value. It workers looking to move from an industry to another is not a minor exploitation as measured by a lower surplus value rate, but simply a greater salary. It is true that for a single company with a fixed degree of mechanization, the greater surplus value the lower the wages, but the reasoning does not extend to different companies in different branches of production, with varying degrees of automation etc. This type of forced homogenization, based on the unrestricted application of the abstraction, can generate distortions in the Marxist theory, which we'll discuss later.

Organic composition of capital

Basically it is the ratio between the constant capital **c** and total capital invested in an enterprise, branch of industry, etc **c+v**. We can express this as:

$$q = c/(c+v)$$

It denotes as the amount of raw materials, equipment and production facilities of an industry as a fraction or percentage of the total capital used, including the above plus labor. It is not the simple relationship of equipment supplied to labor to increase their productivity, as included in **c** is also the value of the materials, which tends to be of dominant magnitude against the depreciation of equipment.

The value of the organic composition of capital depends among others on the following factors:

• The level of wages, the increase of which produces a relative low **q**, since we find **v** in the divisor.

• The quality of equipment, whose increase produces an increase in **q**, since **c** has more preponderance in the dividend that in the divisor.

• The productivity of work, product of the previous item, and that influences decreasing the part of **v** with respect to **c**

• The costs of raw materials, included in **c** and whose growth also produces that of **q**.

Rate of profit (or benefits)

It is undoubtedly a crucial value for the entrepreneur. Marx defines it as the ratio between surplus value and total capital employed in the production of commodities, under the formula:

$$p = s/(c+v)$$

The first point that must be made is that it identifies profit with surplus value, ignoring that the latter does not go entirely to the pocket of the direct employer, since he must pay taxes to the Government and share his cut of surplus value with other businessmen to whom he must pay rent and interest, which are an important part of the total surplus value.

On the other hand, the formula given above may refer to a specific commodity, analyzed individually and punctually, while the concept of profit is usually associated with the benefit that a company gets within a given period, for example an accounting year, quarter, etc. This distinction is important because the capital used in a period is not the simple sum of the capital used to manufacture each of the commodities produced in this period, due to the rotation of the capital. In addition, each factor of production (land, buildings, machinery, raw materials, workmanship etc.) rotates with a different speed. Marx however introduces the hypothesis that all elements of capital rotate with the same speed, and do so once a year or in the chosen period. This abstraction of the different speeds of rotation brings again a distortion that will vary from industry in industry.

Let's see then is the algebraic relationship (if there any) between the three indicators that we have defined here: the rate of surplus value **s'**, the organic composition of capital **q**, and the rate of profit **p**. The reader who is not interested in mathematic demonstrations can safely go directly to the formula denoted by **(A).**

From the definition of rate of profit we multiply dividend and divisor by **v**, which does not alter the equation:

$$\mathbf{p = s/(c+v) = sv/v(c+v),}$$

We then add and subtract sc to the dividend

$$p = sc + sv - sc / v(c+v) = s(c+v) - sc / v(c+v) = s \ (c+v)/ v(c+v) - sc / v(c+v) = s/v - s/v. \ c/(c+v)$$

as $s/v = s`$, y $c/(c+v) = q$ replacing above:

$$p = s' (1-q) \quad (A)$$

We see in this equation that actually the three indicators are related. The relationship can be stated as follows: the increase in the rate of surplus value s' produces an increase of the rate of profit p, while the increase in the organic composition of capital q makes p decrease.

Also in the case of the rate of profit (defined as we have seen) Marx introduces the hypothesis of uniformity in all companies of a certain branch of industry, and between the various branches among themselves. The justification given for this case coincides with the one given for the rate of surplus value, i.e., the migration of capital looking to exit branches of low earnings. However, given the way in which p and s' are linked by the formula **(A),** in that case it also should be uniform the organic composition of capital q among different industries. We can check these assuming two industries (1) and (2). Applying the formula (A) to both we have:

$$P1 = s'1 \ (1 - q1)$$

$$P2 = s'2 \ (1 - q2)$$

If we postulate the equality of rates in all branches, we must:

$$P1=p2$$

$$s'1=s'2$$

This can only be fulfilled if:

$$q1=q2$$

Now, this is not quite the case, and not only there are major differences between organic compositions of capital **q** in different industries, but that there are no signs that there are forces that tend to balance those differences. Indeed, the organic composition of capital intensive industries on the one hand, and labor-intensive industries and services on the other they are widely different, and their equalization cannot be justified.

Marx, who was probably aware of this difficulty, decides however to ignore it and assume an organic composition of capital in all industries since otherwise the results would jeopardize the entire structure of the theory of value.

What has happened here? What effectively has a tendency to get standardized in the real economy is the rate of profit, but not calculated as Marx does it for a commodity in particular and then extrapolating it to throughout a period, but taking into account what was previously observed on the different velocities of rotation of each factor of production. It is due to this trend that capital migrates from obsolete and scarcely profitable industries to others more promising. Neither the organic composition of capital nor the rate of surplus value per se are determinants that may cause the movement of capital from one line to another, but only the possibility of benefits in the annual cycle.

We see therefore how the series of abstractions made by Marx lead to distortions that contradict reality. This will be extended in the following chapters.

CHAPTER 5

Accumulation

The issue of accumulation is absolutely central in the Marxist analysis of capitalism. Once again we will begin this chapter with the study of the simpler case that although unrealistic, should give us an approximation to the object of interest.

Simple reproduction

In the simple reproduction the system under study, a national economy for example, permanently keeps the same size and the same distribution between its different integral parts. This implies that the system replenishes property and equipment worn in the course of the year, without producing additional production means, and that employers consume all the surplus value and workers all their salary in consumer commodities, which are the same period after period.

To guide the analysis, let's assume that the economy is divided into two major sectors, one of manufacturing of production goods (which as we all know includes machinery, installations and raw materials) which we will I, and another II sector producing consumer commodities, both for entrepreneurs and for workers.

By applying the formula of the total value that we saw in previous chapters to each of the sectors we have:

Sector I) $w_1 = c_1 + v_1 + s_1$ (1)

Sector II) $w_2 = c_2 + v_2 + s_2$ (2)

So the value produced in the sector of production commodities is the sum of constant capital used in the same c_1, plus the v_1 wages paid to their workers, plus surplus value earned by its entrepreneur s_1. The same happens in sector II.

Unto the fulfilling of the defining condition of simple reproduction, the value of production commodities created in sector I, according to the formula (1), will be purchased and consumed in the following year by both sectors I and II, i.e., the supply of commodities (1) is identical to the demand of production of both sectors:

$w_1 = c_1 + v_1 + s_1 = c_1 + c_2$ (3)

On the other hand, the total supply of consumer commodities produced by the sector II and reflected by the formula (2), will be entirely consumed by the capitalists of both sectors ($s_1 + s_2$) and workers of the same ($v_1 + v_2$):

$$w2=c2+v2+s2=v1+s1+v2+s2 \quad (4)$$

Simplifying **c1** in both members of equation (3), and v2+s2 in (4), in both cases the following expression is reached:

$$v1+s1=c2 \quad (5)$$

That is to say, that the condition for simple reproduction is that constant capital (machinery, installations and raw materials) used in the consumer commodities sector is equal in value to the sum of the commodities consumed by workers (v1) and capitalists (s1) of the sector of production goods manufacturing. This condition ensures that the economy remains unchanged in time.

As it was expressed, the condition is unrealistic, because it does not even provides for the increase of the quantity of commodities required to meet the population growth, but provides a conceptual framework for the treatment that follows.

The capitalist accumulation

When studying the simple reproduction process we have seen that the capitalist spends all his income from the production process, i.e. surplus value, to maintain his consumption at a constant level. However it is not the lack of increase in this level what interests us, but the fact that the objective of the capitalist seems to be consumption in itself. We have seen in previous chapters that the entrepreneur iterates the economic cycle route

D1-M-D2

Where D2, the amount of money at the end of the cycle, must be greater than the initial amount D1 or otherwise the work of the entrepreneur does not make sense. That is to say that the objective of the capitalist as such can never be consumption but the multiplication of his capital. This feature differentiates it qualitatively of the feudal Lord, one of whose main motivations was to increase his own consumption and that of his court.

The objective of the capitalist to increase his capital is achieved creating a surplus to be able to invest it in the next business cycle, in order to obtain one surplus value greater than in the current cycle, and invest it in turn in the next cycle, and successively increase his worth indefinitely.

We have thus defined the essence of the process of accumulation in its main feature, and we say that this is the driving force of the capitalist system, from which derives all its momentum and transforming power.

Logically, a part of surplus value s that the entrepreneur obtains from his workers in a given business cycle, may be effectively used it meet his personal needs and those of his family and dependents, so that there is always in each individual pattern competition between his tendency to consume and his willingness to save and reinvest. The classical economists called this the "principle of abstinence", according to which the capitalist sacrifices himself abstaining from consuming to be able to re-invest those savings in the production process. Marx mocks this virtuous trait on the grounds that in reality what the capitalist seeks is to increase the amount of people that he exploits, and therefore his position and prestige in the society, which depends only on the amount of its capital, and that is this, and not the increased consumption which produces him pleasure. No matter what we think of the subjective reasons of the entrepreneur, which surely will vary from person to person, the fact is that the growth of the economy as a whole depends critically on that business owners repeatedly roam the D1-M-D2 cycle and reinvest most of their profits in their business. The replacement of individual capitalists by shareholders and their managers at the head of large and medium-sized enterprises does not change this pattern, but confirms the trends exposed, since they do not proceed according to individual desires, but according to their role within the mentioned cycle D1-M-D2.

Public companies also seek to make a profit, in such a way to increase their size and power to serve an increasing number of users and customers, and at the same time providing a more extended and better performance.

The industrial reserve army

According to the theory of Marx, the value of the labor force is given by the amount of means of subsistence necessary for maintaining the worker and his family. That is an equilibrium value at which the salary will be reestablished if there has been a deviation due to some circumstantial reason

The accumulation process increases the requirements of the various factors involved in the process of production, in particular of the labor force. In general, due to the law of supply and demand, which Marx acknowledges, by increasing the demand for a particular good its price will go up, until the opportunity offered to entrepreneurs to make an gain produces a migration of investments into the production of the good with an increased demand, raising its volume and producing a downward trend, to restore the pre-existing balance, so that the price will again converge to its value. But this reasoning, valid for raw materials and machinery, does not work for the labor force; the fact that wages will rise will not produce an increase of the population or offer extra labor force within a commensurate period of business cycles- except cases of human migration that do exist, but this is a relocation rather than a net increase- so salaries will rise above the value of the commodities.

This is a serious violation of the theory of value, and just takes place in one of its main components. Since the accumulation of capital is permanent, the price of labor (i.e. wages) would always tend to exceed its value in a progressive way. There is no doubt that this finding represents a challenge to any theory of value of Marx.

Our author reacts with the application of what he calls the labor reserve army. A part of the population that would like to get a job fails to do so and the mere existence of this surplus of labor supply presses wages downwards, counteracting the upward pressure created by the accumulation and their ever-growing needs of labor. The origin of this army of unemployed people has several sources according to the historical circumstances of each society: on the one hand it's peasant population that migrates to the cities looking for better living conditions, or pushed by hunger, drought, agricultural pests, persecution or war; This process of urbanization has certainly created surplus of labor supply throughout the history of humanity, and has been the source of the first contingents of factory workers.

On the other hand, the introduction of machinery replaces labor, feeding that reserve army on a permanent basis. Each entrepreneur tries to increase his individual productivity, and the combined effect of these decisions is the displacement of labor in times of crisis, or the slower absorption of the same in good times. In this way, capitalism prevents the disappearance of the surplus value- which otherwise would be in danger of being absorbed by the permanent wage increases- and accomplishes the self preservation of the system.

At this point corresponds to make two comments on this process, always following Marx: on the one hand, the replacement of labor by machinery has the effect of increasing the organic composition of capital, growing **c** at the expense of **v**, according to the nomenclature previously used. This has consequences which will be discussed later, in the context of the theory of the capitalist crisis. On the other hand, if for some reason (for example, the emergence of a new industry or the colonization of a new territory or business niche) there is a significant increase in the demand for labor, surplus value will decrease in favor of variable capital; This will have the effect of reducing the rate of accumulation and put a brake on the process of increase in the demand for workers: in this way, there is a kind of self-regulating mechanism for the maintenance of the reserve army, and therefore preservation of surplus value. We will also return to this topic when dealing with the capitalist crisis.

Classical economic theory, formulated in the same time frame as Malthusianism, and at a time of strong population growth in Europe by introduction of sanitary measures with the consequent reduction of mortality, envisaged that the compensation that would limit the indefinite growth of wages due to the process of capitalist accumulation would be precisely the increase in labor supply, fruit of this demographic growth. So that to counter the fall in the rate of profit, he proposed a population argument. The explanatory power of this theory declined significantly when the population growth in the core countries stabilized at lower rates.

Marx, although did not disdain the population argument, provided an additional explanation for the limitation of the level of wages: the self-regulatory mechanism provided by the industrial reserve army, explained by the capitalist development itself independently of external demographic theories. The employed labor mass and reserve army are at all times in a position of unstable balance, which changes with the economic climate of bonanza feeding the first at the expense of the second, or depression, with the reverse effect. We can think of the employed labor mass and reserve army as two interconnected compartments, and through the connection there will be a flow of workers from one to the other compartment according to the economic atmosphere of prosperity or depression of the time.

On the other hand, technological change ceases to be for Marx an unpredictable and random effect that may or not occur, and becomes a link that is indispensable for the maintenance of the reserve army and therefore the rate of surplus value.

In addition the changes in production methods- as part of what Marx calls infrastructure- modify the institutional and ideological superstructure of society. The causal relationship is the following: changes in production methods originate economic and social changes among the members of the community, and both institutional coverage and the way that society views itself are modified at the same time accordingly. From there emerges his well known and luminous phrase that the "anatomy of civil society must be sought in the political economy".

As in the previous cases, it is pertinent to wonder about the validity and relevance of the proposal of Marx on the issues raised in this chapter, in particular on the reserve army. Within his claims there are actually several incontrovertible facts: the existence of unemployment in different proportions is a constant of the capitalist system and so is the fact that technological progress destroys jobs. The depressive effect of unemployment on the income of all workers is also a reality.

What happens is that unlike the feudal stage, each person does not have a fixed role as serf, or some other form of bondage, which on the one hand deprived him of any possibility of emancipation or improvement, but on the other guaranteed him a gray existence but with fewer surprises. In capitalism, particularly in its initial and medium times in which Marx wrote, there is no containment network and each is rid to their fate. The counterpart of the absence of a (at least theoretical) ceiling to the possibilities is the lack of (often brutally real) floor.

There are no privileges of medieval guilds, with their market reserves: everything is subject to competition and change, and in this society there are no everlasting guarantees. Few of the leading companies of any segment of business at the end of the 19th century arrived undamaged at present time; the process of digestion of companies is fierce and permanent.

With the modern advent of globalization, this has been aggravated by the massive transfer of millions of jobs to other geographic areas that until recently were not competing for them, with its load of anxieties and unemployment which produces the loss of employment, in general in Western countries.

It is also true that employers try to replace as much labor as possible by machines, not as an action specifically targeted at the working class, but within a general plan of cost reduction that encompasses not only to the labor force, but raw materials, other materials, energy and services, etc. In reality, if they do so to increase their prestige in society as holders of capital, or out of necessity of survival is questionable.

But to see the full panorama we should check what the consequences of these actions at the global level have been: all kinds of commodities, previously produced for small wealthy layers, are produced now for huge masses of consumers, including primarily the workers, at affordable prices for many of them. Although in the production of each unit of any type of commodities there is now lower labor content, the scales of production multiplied to infinity have created permanent new jobs, in many cases of greater value than the previous ones. Most brutal works have precisely been replaced by machines, and the degree of physical exploitation that was previously the norm is no longer permissible. Slave work, work of children and other human miseries still subsist, but as exceptions which in general are chased by society in the majority of countries but unfortunately not at all.

The counterpart of the disappearance of jobs in the West was the creation of hundreds of millions of them in the Far East, in countries that were not included in the productive world map, nor were their population included in the consumers map.

The big social problem today is the situation of those who fail to get a job, the marginalized, rather than the overexploitation of the proletariat.

Value and price II

As we have seen in Chapter 3 concerning value, Marx used his concept of value in all their reasoning and mathematical developments, resulting sometimes an anti intuitive practice since in general typically discussions are in terms of the prices which the commodities reach effectively in their respective markets. We have already explained that the author tries to calm the cravings that this change may cause in people arguing that prices, subject to ups and downs due to multiple causes, tend however to gravitate towards the respective values once these accidental causes fade away. Although the cost of labor is an important factor in pricing, it is difficult to check if such convergence occurs in practice, particularly in our current economy, marked by a huge amount of new technology-based products.

Within the political economy of Marx, there is another factor to keep in mind: quantities based on the value succeed to account for certain clearly verifiable trends, in particular the tendency to homogenize the rates of profits among different branches of the industry, caused by the migration of capital from low to other more profitable areas.

To explain theoretically this empirical verification, Marx raises a number of formulas based on the value, as we have defined it, dividing companies for this purpose in three large compartments: one dedicated to the production of production means, of what is called constant capital; a second sector produces consumer commodities for workers, which make up the variable capital, and a third sector produces commodities for the capitalist class, luxury commodities. To maintain the consistency of the system on a hypothesis of simple reproduction, he equals the sum of the goods produced by the first sector with the sum of constant capital of the three sectors, so that constant capital assets produced match the needs of the entire economy, which is the condition of simple reproduction. The same applies to the other two sectors. He then raises a number of equations of tedious development, which we do not reproduce to maintain the reader's interest. Keeping the condition that the organic composition of capital is the same in all three branches the equations give correct results, and are compatible with the trend towards uniform profits in these rates, but as soon as this unrealistic hypothesis is abandoned the mentioned profit rates differ in form that is directly proportional to the divergence among organic compositions. This is in flagrant contradiction with the experimental findings of a tendency to uniformity in the profit rate **simultaneously** with the divergence of the organic composition of capital.

This is a major failure in the theory, which casts doubt on the entire law of value work. Marx seems to have been aware of the problem and tried a solution that proved to be unsatisfactory. His followers have tested numerous theories to save the problem, but are so complex that it is difficult to judge their validity; ultimately it cannot be considered that the issue is resolved.

Why the insistence of Marx in defining everything based on the value? The answer is that in this way he tries to put in evidence that a portion of the value, created according to the author only by labor, is not paid to the working class but it is appropriated by the capitalists. In this way it allows him to define profit rate according to the surplus value rate, implying that surplus value is the only source of profit, while working with prices would lead to define the gain as a result of all the capital, not just of the variable part. In short, Marx sacrificed the mathematical validity of his reasoning for the sake of his basic purpose that as we have seen is to show the exploitation of the proletariat by the capitalist class.

SECOND PART

Capitalist crisis

Although it is generally recognized the contribution Marx made to the treatment of the economic crises of capitalism, there is no centralized and systematic analysis of the issue, for example in the volumes of Capital. A probable reason is that the volumes II and III did not have the correction of Marx and contain important but not full material. It is likely that, having lived longer, Marx would have devoted time and energy to this aspect.

Instead there are numerous mentions and fragmentary treatments in Capital and other works written by him, which induced his successors to try to fill the void using concepts developed by the German author.

In general he described crises as situations in which producers cannot place among its clients part of their products that accumulate forming stocks which finally have no possibility of its realizing their value. When they experience this lack of sales, the entrepreneurs stop in turn buying inputs and hiring labor, increasing the crisis as a number of potential consumers will not have resources to buy. On the surface it's a crisis of overproduction, but that appearance is misleading, since it is not that each producer has necessarily produced more commodities than usual, but that for some reason, sectors of consumers stop buying:

M1-D-M2-D-M3-D......

It is important to note that the decision of one of the links not to buy - and therefore refrain from producing - interrupts a whole chain of transactions. If this behavior extends to broad economic sectors, we are in the presence of a crisis of overproduction of all those links prior to the" broken bridge".

In the barter economy, this behavior is not possible, since producer 1 can only sell his commodity to producer 2 if at the same time he purchases his product 2. We will later see in which context such events can occur.

Say's law

The French economist Jean Baptiste Say formulated a law on this subject, which was implicitly accepted by the rest of his contemporary classical economists. In the process of capitalism the transformation of commodities **M** in money **D** and its transformation back into commodities **M** is constant, since it is the essence of the accumulation. Say assigned to this process the status of automatic and inescapable. According to his law, to any sale follows necessarily an equivalent purchase, so an interruption of the sequence M-D-M cannot happen, and therefore a crisis of overproduction is not possible. In other words, he extrapolated a condition of the economy of barter to capitalism.

Marx rightly criticized this law, arguing that the fact that money separates the sequence **M-D- M** in two different sub-sequences: **M1-D**, and **D-M2** which may occur simultaneously or separately, in the same or in different site, causing then the possibility that the second purchase is skipped, is to say that the producer 1 saves his money and producer 2 does not sell his product. Strictly speaking, this reasoning applies not only to capitalism, but to previous systems that used money. It is precisely money that allows separating sales and subsequent purchases at differentiated transactions that can be remote in time and space.

The analysis should determine what the causes of that interruption in the supply chain were. In a few cases the reasons are obvious: war, natural disasters, hindrances to trade and movement of commodities by different causes, etc. But this is not the general situation, and therefore not all the crises in the history can be explained by them.

We get a solid track once again of the comparative analysis of the sequences of simple production and capitalist production. The sequence of transactions in the first, as we said, is M-D- M, where although the commodities of the beginning and end are physically different, they are similar from the point of view of their value, since we assume that participants of barter exchange their products in an equitable manner, since they are well informed about their relative values; the essential thing is to recognize that the purpose of this exchange is the consumption of those things which each producer cannot produce by himself, so the transaction cycle ends with M, a commodity, and this happens for both producers. That's why, in principle there is no reason why one of them to stop producing and selling, since he needs to consume permanently.

On the other hand, in the capitalist production for the market the cycle is:

$$D1\text{-}M\text{-}D2$$

The capitalist starts with a sum of money, transforms it in constant capital and wages producing a commodity M and then sell it to a D2 amount which must be higher than D1, what we symbolized as:

$$D2\text{-}D1 = Delta\ D$$

It is important to highlight that the diversity of attitudes between the capitalist and the employee does not come from ethical sources, nor from an alleged different education received, or any other subjective element, but its objective position within the mentioned cycle M-D-M, i.e. how he begins the cycle and how he is expecting to finish it.

The expectation of our entrepreneur is that Delta D is positive, and that it has a certain magnitude, particularly compared with capital initial D1, i.e. that the rate of profit, which we define in this case by the ratio:

Profit rate=Delta D/ D1= (D2-D1)/ D1

(Which is usually expressed as a percentage)

The capitalist then expects that it will have a certain value; otherwise, that is if his expectations are that he will not obtain that target rate, he may decide not to risk the initial capital D1 in uncertain or even dubious circumstances. This is completely different from our simple producer attitude; the employer can choose to sit on his money and not producing, and therefore not to buy further raw materials or capital commodities or hire workers. Therein lays the seed of crisis.

It should be noted that it is not necessary that the profit rate thus defined is negative or null to trigger the termination of purchases and productions by some of the entrepreneurs. It will be enough that the actual or predicted rate to be less than the target rate, as we called it above, for the capitalists decide not to risk their capital. This has been the explanation of Marx, and in fact, most modern economists have given a convergent explanation. To this end they divide the profit-that is to say the surplus value - in two main areas: the rate of profit of the entrepreneur as a producer itself, and the rate of interest in the use of capital, whether this capital is provided by other capitalists in the financial area, as if it is usual in the case of the industrial entrepreneur, or if he invests his own money, in which case he is taking on two different roles, each one of which has its reward (profit and interest). If the profit rate that the capitalist expect to get in his sale is below or does not exceed the rate of interest that must be paid by the money, he can refrain from committing the own or foreign capital in business and wait for better times. Generalizing this attitude we have a crisis in the making.

Types of Crisis

Marx did not make a classification of the crisis according to their causes, for the reason explained at the beginning: the incomplete nature of their work. His successors were particularly active in systematizing the analysis left by the author to explain the economic crises of capitalism and predict its future development. Of the various existing classifications, we will select one that divides crisis into two categories, each of them in turn divisible into two subcategories.

• The first category is that of the so-called crisis due to reduction of the rate of return, in which the rate of surplus value and therefore the profit suffer a reduction, either by: 1) the increase in wages above their value (determined as we saw before, by the time needed to produce the means of subsistence of the workers), which produces directly a reduction in the rate of surplus value, 2) the declining trend of the rate of profit, caused by the increase in the organic composition of capital, as we shall see in more detail in a chapter dedicated to it.

• The second of these categories is usually called crisis of realization, determined by the impossibility of the productive system of selling its production-or at least a substantial part of it - to its value, which must be liquidated at prices below its value, or remain in stock and finally become obsolete. Also in this case, one can discern two different reasons for the occurrence of such a crisis of realization. The first gives rise to the so-called crisis of under-consumption. caused by the impossibility of economic operators, particularly the members of the working class, of consuming the production carried out in certain cycles, due simply to the lack of revenue to make carry on this consumption. The second cause within this kind of crisis is that called for mismatch or disproportionality. The same would be produced by the random and seemingly anarchic character of production within the capitalist system, where there is no authority setting production quotas to different agents: this would lead to the sub or overproduction of certain commodities, either capital or consumption goods, by lack of information at the time the productions are programmed by the individual capitalists who are unrelated among themselves.

We will see the main of these grounds in successive chapters.

CHAPTER 6

Crisis by decrease of the rate of profit I

Increase in the organic composition of capital

The classical economists had assigned to capitalism the historical mission of developing the productive forces of society to its maximum expression, which has indeed fulfilled largely, so they saw with concern what perceived as signs of a downward trend in the general profit rate, which is the ultimate reason that moves entrepreneurs to carry out their tasks, and therefore constitutes the fuel of the system. Adam Smith and David Ricardo and even the more modern John Maynard Keynes noted this trend and expressed their fears. They were on the one hand based on some reasoning and mathematical developments of the type that we will see below, and on the other in thoughts of the pessimistic atmosphere of the Malthusianism.

Marx developed his own theory on the subject, and assigned it great importance in the context of all his conceptual work, to the point of defining it as the most important law of political economy, though he was aware of the factors limiting its effects, as we will see.

To present in a simple way the law of the downward trend in the rate of profit of Marx, we will depart from the equation already deduced:

$$p = s'(1-q)$$

As we have seen, this equation relates among them the profit **p** with the surplus value rate **s'** and the organic composition of the capital **q.** We have already mentioned the undeniable growing trend that **q** has, due to the introduction of more machinery in lieu of workmanship which produced a marked increase in productivity, and also by the ever-growing quantities of raw material that those production means can process. In other words the two components of q have a clearly upward trend over time. As **q** is subtracting in the equation, its growth will produce mathematically a decrease in the rate of profit **p**. The straightforward conclusion of this formula as it is expressed is both clear and crucial: the very development of capitalism creates conditions that set limits to its expansion, via putting a brake to its engine: profit. This would justify the fears of the classical economists and would put an expiration date to the system.

We have seen that the surplus value is divided into three parts (aside from what the State detracts as taxes): the gain of the capitalist entrepreneur himself, the interest that he pays for the use of capital, and the rent paid for the use of land. With the fall of the rate of profit, all of them end up being affected, as well as the payment of taxes.

As we said, there are a number of factors which limit the real scope of validity of this law, of which Marx was aware, and of which he lists six. We will mention only the most important of them:

• Decrease in the unit value of constant capital: since the introduction of machinery considerably raises labor productivity, the value content of each unit of constant capital (raw material, materials and equipment) descends. That means that growth in terms of value (or from the content of necessary work) of constant capital is less than the increase in physical volume, which limits the global growth of **c** and therefore **q**, thus benefiting **p**

• Increase of the rate of surplus value by various means: extension of the working day (not so much in the present days, but feasible in the time of Marx), decrease of wages below its value using the increase in the army's reserve, etc. A particular case is the increase of productivity by greater mechanization, which while it increases the organic composition of capital also has an impact on the surplus value. This effect can be checked by reiterating the formula that relates them.

$$p = s^{`}(1 - q)$$

Which shows that any increase in **s** ' raises the value of **p,** although it has been originated in an increase of **q** (that's if decreases **p**).

• International trade: it permits to incorporate commodities manufactured using cheaper labor, because in some countries the means of subsistence are cheaper than in the industrial powers. In addition, from peripheral countries cheap food imports depresses the cost of living in the central countries lowering the value of the variable capital through the reduction the cost of subsistence.

Analysis of the law

Recognizing these limitations to the declining trend of the rate of profit, Marx argued that it had effect only over long periods of time, covering numerous business cycles. This is equivalent to say that the law exists though it may not be easy to check its operation, since we will not know if the period of study has been sufficiently long.

Having done a detailed analysis on this issue we will ask once more that it can be concluded on the so-called law of the declining trend of the rate of profit made by Marx. Is it a real and verifiable effect though only verifiable in very long periods as finally argued Marx, or has flaws that invalidate it?

To give an answer we should consider once again the formula that relates the three main variables, **p, s'** and **q**.

$$p = s`(1-q)$$

This equation allows us to say mathematically is that when q grows, if everything else remains constant, the profit **p** rate will decrease.

In this context, the key expression is "if everything else remains constant"; everything else here is **s'**. Can we safely assume that **s'** will remain constant when **q** goes up? The answer is frankly negative. We cannot assume that **s'** will remain constant or that it will descend when **q** grows. The reason is that the main purpose of incorporating modern machinery (i.e. to increase **q**) is to save labor, so the surplus value will grow against **v**, and therefore the surplus value rate will grow too. So the only realistic scenario is to forecast simultaneous increases in **s'** (which will increase **p**) and in **q** (which decreases it). At first glance it would seem that it is necessary to know what will be the growth of **s'** and **q** to evaluate which will have a bigger impact in **p** fixation. In fact we don't have. Decisions to buy machinery and technology in general are taken by employers according to their impact on costs; will buy only those means that raise them the profit rate, whatever its mathematical formulation. In this way, there does not exist in the mathematical expression a reason to foresee a declining rate of the surplus value or the profit, at least as a consequence of the increase in the organic composition of capital. The law enunciated by Marx does not have a correlation with reality. What the author correctly had enunciated as a limiting factor (see above) actually invalidates the law in practice.

This is a widespread feature in Marxism: Marx set out his laws deterministically, as events that will necessarily occur dragging all the characters as in a Greek tragedy. It does not take into account that each micro or macro decision is made by men who know their businesses and made their calculations in the most realistic way possible. It is precisely this decentralized characteristic of capitalism which has given it the necessary plasticity to have survived to our time.

In fact, aside from accounting fluctuations in the profit margins of companies measured as usual, the total mass of surplus value obtained by capitalist companies as a whole grows every year, except for the periods of crisis. It is this fact that motorizes the secular trend of companies stock rising prices in the world stock markets, once the effect of inflation is discounted. The remarkable increase in worldwide productive economy since Marx´s times has been permanently fed by these profits.

CHAPTER 7

Crisis by decrease of the rate of profit II

Decrease of surplus value

We have seen in the previous chapter that the basis for a theory of the crisis based on the reduction of the rate of profit by increase in the organic composition of capital is feeble and in any case a marginal element. But this is not the only cause of crisis by lowering the rate of profit that Marx conceived. In his writings there is not a strict separation of causes as we are considering here, but is has been his followers who have separated the causes for elaborating on them.

Marx sees another causal crisis in the sustained increase in wages, causing a decline in surplus value, or at least the rate of surplus value $s`=s/v$. The sequence of reasoning is as follows: the accumulation process permanently produces surplus of capital from surplus value taken to workers; these funds need to be reinvested to meet the goals of the capitalists that as we have seen, is always expanding their equity by incorporating immediately surplus value to their capital, in order to produce more surplus value, etc.

This compels them to add more machinery and raw materials, i.e. more capital in their companies, but also to always hire more labor, enlarging the variable capital. As there is a reserve army, they can recruit more workers without problems and incorporate them into their payroll. As on the other hand the mechanization and automation of work leave unemployed workers, this reserve army renews on a permanent basis. However there is no guarantee that the rate of unemployed workers by mechanization matches the pace of new hires by expansion of production. The reserve army effectively decreases in numbers in certain circumstances in which societies are approaching full employment. It rarely occurs that unemployment reaches zero, since part of the population seeking work is actually difficult unemployable due to lack of training or other reasons, and in addition there is a frictional unemployment of people changing from work to another. What is really important is whether the unemployment rate is significantly lower compared to its usual levels. This, which is good news from the social point of view, would be to Marx bad news for capitalists, since they must compete among them to be able to hire the workforce they need, particularly when they require certain levels of training. Competition for labor is reflected in an increase in wages above their value (defined as we have seen in the first chapters), so that in the formation of total value that we have defined as **w**, grows the part corresponding to the variable capital **v** at the expense of the surplus value **s**. Marx notes that overproduction crises are often paradoxically preceded by periods of high wages. In this way, the crises of this type would respond to the following sequence:

Accumulation=> investment => higher employment rate=> depletion of the industrial reserve army=> higher salaries=>drop in the surplus value and profit rates=>crisis.

The efficient reason of crises of this type would be the same that was exposed for all crises: capitalists, dissatisfied with their current profit rate, lose their interest in investing and consequently withdraw their capital from the production market.

We have to notice - this is a remarkable Marx's contribution- that crises of this type do not originate by random processes, or erratic and accidental causes, but are a result of the normal capitalist development itself, and that is why accumulation- i.e. a normal business fact- appears first in the previous sequence. Marx deals then with the unfolding of the crisis thus generated: important parts of the invested capital are unproductive or its value is destroyed, starting with appropriations of creditors who may not collect their money, the chain of payments gets broken on countless sites, commodities may not be sold at their values but at big discounts, inactive production commodities lose their value and finally workers no longer find employment so they have accept whatever they can get and real wage level drops below what it had been at the beginning of the cycle. The crucial point is that as all the components of the capital acting as costs are depreciated, the profit rate returns to climb and to seem attractive.

Ultimately, the balance is restored destroying value for all members of the market. Supreme irrationality!

As we have seen, once the crisis is unleashed its course can also be represented by a scheme similar to that wrote its gestation:

Crisis=> value destruction of all assets=> salary drop=>improvement of surplus value and profit rates =>beginning of a new cycle=> accumulation.

What brings us back to the starting point of the previous scheme.

A very well founded question may be considered at this point: being that ultimately the crisis will erode his assets, devalue his products and put him out of business for a while, why does the capitalist choose to follow the signals of his declining rate of profit and not reinvest, limited to expect future better rates, rather than endure the shower and continue in business with all his strength avoiding the outbreak of the crisis? This question, seemingly logical and somewhat suggested by the same approach which makes Marx, ignores the difference between levels of individual and collective decision and action: the capitalist is not actually speculating with the decline in wages and the rise in surplus value which will follow should a crisis occur, but he is watching his market and detecting unequivocal signals that he will be able to sell his commodity to a remunerative price, and then decides to withdraw from the market or at least of the reinvestment; from his individual point of view this is the rational decision to prevents losses. What happens is that when many capitalists operating in different markets take the same decision simultaneously, this decision causes the crisis with its destruction of value for all players.

An important point: the crisis is no longer for Marx an isolated event, but the specific way to restore markets to normal, i.e. it is an integral part and necessary for each cycle in capitalism. For this reason rather than a theory of crises we are facing a theory of the business cycle. Indeed, the crisis is a phase of the cycle, and capitalism is a relentless series of cycles.

Even though this is the conclusion obtained from the theory of crises of Marx, many subsequent non Marxist economists came to similar conclusions, after making descriptions of the development of crises similar in many respects to those described here. The main difference seems to be in their visualization of the impact of crises on the future of capitalism. While Marx and his followers always interpreted that crises were the pre-announcement of the final collapse of the system, non Marxist economists, significantly Schumpeter- whose theories we will give a short description later - considered that the is the normal form of capitalist development; in this view, crises are a mechanism, painful but necessary, to self-purging system, in which non-viable industries, unskilled capitalists and obsolete assets are eliminated. Both theses share a somewhat Darwinian worldview.

There is no doubt that much of the treatment of crises that Marx makes is correct and current, but before anticipating conclusions we must still study other causes of economic crises, which we have collectively called crisis of realization.

CHAPTER 8

Crisis by disproportionality

In capitalism there is no central authority in individual countries or in the system as a whole, ordering the various variables of production and consumption, such as types of products, quantities and temporary production plans, prices, etc. Each production unit carries out its estimates of sales and proceeds to make their production schedules accordingly. This can cause mistakes with regard to the consumption of certain commodities, their geographical distribution and temporal preferences of consumers, determination of their purchase power, availability of skilled labor, raw materials and other factors of production, etc. This can result in big mistakes in quantities, quality and prices, and often causes the impossibility of placing all the production in accessible markets, or conversely scarcity and shortages of commodities, collapse of prices, unsold products that become obsolete, financial difficulties for having frozen assets and ultimately, wasteful of resources.

One of the classic examples of mismatches that can occur is between the quantities of final commodities required by the market and the availability of the corresponding raw materials. Obviously the relative scarcity of just one of them fixes an impassable limit to the production of the final good, unless there can be a replacement of the material that creates the bottleneck by other relatively more abundant, what is sometimes possible. By the way, there are cases where the replacement of inputs is not feasible at suitable costs, so the final commodities prices grow over time. This is the case of the oil, where alternative energy sources are not yet in position to take the lead.

If markets were relatively stable on their commodities requirements, eventually the mismatches could be quantified and corrected, which would eliminate the cause of this kind of crisis. In fact, the most outstanding feature of capitalism is its state of permanent imbalance created by competition, in which new players try to dislodge the existing, or already present producers try to expand their market share at the expense of its competitors. How can it be that imbalances do not take increasing dimensions, get out of control and jeopardize the macro-stability of the system?

The answer is that there is an internal mechanism which tends to return the system closer to the equilibrium positions... until the next challenge.

The mechanism, one of the expressions of the "invisible hand" of Adam Smith, is the fact that if the additional demand created in a special sector by an unforeseen increase in consumption for any reason is not satisfied, it originates higher commodity prices, proportional to the extent of shortages. Capitalists from other areas of lower profitability will soon detect opportunities for extras profit that originate elsewhere and migrate with their capitals to the area in question, by increasing production and therefore offer, with which the price will be gradually placed in a strip of balance with the rest of the economy prices. The reasoning that we have done with prices is also valid with values and the result will be the same.

Crises as described have occurred in branches of business and certain countries. As a consequence, countless firms of all sizes are going bankrupt all the time and contingent of employees go out of work for that reason.

With the advance of the statistics and the dissemination of information, the rise of marketing techniques and segmentation of customers needs at an increasingly finer level, flexible production planning techniques and commercial monitoring etc., although planning errors cannot be eliminated, their effects can be limited reacting in time to turn the tide, in such a way of mitigating the impact of such errors on the firms, employment and society as a whole.

The alternative fixing production method has been the socialist central planning, as it was practiced for decades by the former Soviet Union and the Communist bloc countries; therein a bureaucrat in Moscow determined the production plan of factories in the Kamchatka peninsula, at seven time zones of distance, and these plans were unshakable since they had traveled approval process by all kinds of technical and political instances, so once launched a plan carefully designed and implemented, there was no way to stop it despite the despair of men in the industrial or commercial front line. It produced not only one even greater resource wastage, but it its more harmful effect was to plunge into an atmosphere of comfort, reluctant to changes that could cause risks, which acted as a very efficient brake to the innovations, which are driven by unbridled competition in a free economy. The immense variety of products of all kinds available to consumers in countries within the capitalist sphere contrasts with the gloomy monotony and the long queues for most basic purchases that prevailed in the Communist countries, and still nowadays in Cuba and Venezuela. The rejection to return to that grey life acted as a spur in the ex Communist countries to get through the hard processes of transformation of their socialist economies in market or hybrid economies.

In fact, Marx never devoted much long time or energy to this kind of crisis. Its specific and always changing character hinder their treatment within the framework of general laws as those stated by Marx. It was rather some of his disciples who attempted to develop a theory on the subject, but always had a somewhat marginal character, and some authors, Marxist or not, consider them like an additional disturbing factor of crises triggered by of other causes rather than their true roots.

In the last two decades there have been speculative origin crisis centered in certain areas of the economy, especially in the area of construction and real estate, financial with the emergence of new and very aggressive instruments, certain luxury goods, etc. Although the stock market speculation existed in the time of Marx, these present crises have innovative elements. It has already been said that real crises have components of many of the types mentioned above, and it is legitimate to wonder if these speculative crisis have a strong bias of mismatch or disproportionality. Indeed, watching the crisis real estate of the past decade in the United States, Spain and other countries, which then spread to other activities in concentric waves, had origins in imbalances between resources focused on the real estate activity for example compared with the past proportion of resources devoted to it, mismatches between the quantity and cost of housing and the purchasing power of potential buyers, and finally imbalance between the value of the same and market prices. An investigation into such crisis would throw light on its causes and would be timely since they have high probability of appearing recurrently.

CHAPTER 9

Under consumption crisis

Marx and his followers explained that there is a fundamental contradiction between the purposes of the production as a process of creation of use values, and the end of capitalism as a process of creation of exchange value. Consumption is which provides the impulse to the production giving it an object, and even the manufacture of production means has as last purpose to use these means to create consumer commodities.

This contradiction is reflected, according to Marx, in precursory behaviors of typical crisis of under-consumption.

Indeed, capitalists seek to permanently expand the rate of surplus value, which can be achieved only at the expense of the variable capital, i.e. the wage. They rarely achieve this goal decreasing the nominal level of remuneration, somewhat more frequently limiting its growth, for example by introducing more and better machines that replace labor and fuelling the reserve army. But in so doing, they hinder the expansion of markets keeping outside them potentially consuming sectors, or curbing their purchasing power. In this way, while on the one hand new production is injected permanently to the aforementioned markets, on the other hand demand growth is prevented in such a way that the extra supply cannot be absorbed. After a time in which this development manifests, the generation of an unmarketable surplus of commodities is inexorable, and from there a crisis of overproduction caused by under-consumption is just around the corner. It is something like driving an auto stepping on the accelerator while brakes are applied at the same time. This behavior, seemingly schizophrenic, is perfectly in accordance with the laws of capitalism.

Marx explains that, while only the consumption can give a justification to the production, capitalism permanently presses to increase production without the consideration of an increase in consumption. The complete cycle is composed of two parts: in the first physical production is carried on and so the exploitation manifests by generating surplus value, which occurs independently of what happens in the subsequent stage. But then, in order to get his capital back increased by the profit arising out of the surplus value, the entrepreneur must effectively sell his products, for which he requires the existence of a solvent demand in the marketplace. The generation of surplus value and its effective realization occur in distinct acts, separated in time and space. The first is governed by the productive power of society and the second by their consumption capacity. Imbalances between both give rise to under consumption crises.

Thus, Marx argued that the poverty of the masses and their consequent under consumption constrain capital to a situation of almost permanent underutilization of their installed capacity, only interrupted by periods of euphoria that finally culminate in a crisis of overproduction.

Marx´s analysis is correct and reflects the simple fact that variable capital and surplus value compete for the portion of the value of a product that remains after subtracting the constant capital used from the selling price, and that the bigger one the smaller will be the other. In times of our author the typical worker's compensation was insufficient and forced him to pass hardship and hunger. The situation remains so in sectors, countries and regions of the world today, but it is undeniable that in the West and in increasingly large areas of the East this situation has changed radically, and masses have entered the consumer society, to the point that in fact one of the criticisms that are made to communities in the present times is their propensity to an empty consumerism devoid of values.

What has happened in the past century and half, a relatively short time to explain social mutations so deep and extended in space? Without going into deep economic or sociological analysis, we will say that the change has been a product of two main factors.

• Organized trade union and political action of workers in a permanent struggle to improve their standard of living, through the extension of their participation in the total income of their respective national societies.

• Analyses of the crisis carried out by economists, officials and politicians, who, using different tools than the ones Marx had, came to the same conclusions as he: capitalism has no future if it does not incorporate the masses to the consumption.

This has brought an unprecedented situation a couple of generations ago: countless new products of technological origin and their respective trade policies are designed from the start overlooking their immediate dissemination in mass markets, which obviously includes policy of prices, advertising campaigns and creation of commercial channels suitable for this purpose. We will expose again the limitation of this model: those sectors excluded from employment and consumption, which do not receive wages or generate surplus value, and that for this reason they are often invisible.

...

Made this important exception, the constant incorporation of masses to consumption remains as a characteristic of our times. This has been possible by the plasticity of the capitalist system allowing it to absorb economic and social significant changes without losing its essential features.

Does the tendency to overproduction get solved with the addition of the workers to consumption? Or after this step forward to consumption of masses the causes of under consumption (= overproduction) continue acting despite the improvement of the living conditions of employees?

There have been many discussions in the Marxism about this topic, and several models that sought to justify one response or the other. We will post here the reasoning of Paul Sweezy, which we deem convincing and whose findings coincide with those observable in reality. We reproduce the substance of this reasoning using our own notation.

1. Sweezy subdivides the use of surplus value obtained by capitalists in four parts:

• The first aimed at increasing their consumption.

• The second to increase the pay of their workers.

• The third to hire additional amounts of labor, i.e. to expand the variable capital.

• The last to buy more machinery, which integrates the constant capital.

The third and fourth items are within the process of accumulation, as defined by Marx. Sweezy calls investment only to the forth, in accordance with the usual name in economy (specifically it would be investment in fixed assets).

We will call A the sum of the first and second items growth rates, which represents the pace of the increase in the growth of the consumption of the entire population (capitalists and workers). We will call B to the growth rate of the fourth item, namely investment in means of production.

The reasoning is as follows: the ultimate goal of business is to generate maximum surplus value and with it permanently expand its capital. For this reason they will seek by all means to make accumulation grow more rapidly than total consumption. In addition, the capitalist will try to constantly replace labor with machinery, to feed the reserve army, as it was explained before. This implies that the rate of investment will grow faster that the rate of accumulation, of which is an integral part. With these arguments in mind, we can conclude that the ratio A/B will have a decreasing value over time.

If we call C the growth rate of the production of consumer commodities (which is the final object of the entire production process) and relate to the rate of growth in investment B, the C/B ratio will have a relatively stable trend at the time, or in any case will not be a downward trend, since the increase in investment in the accumulation allows to ensure at least the constancy of productivity. We will then relate the previous ratios in the following way:

$$\underline{A/B}$$

$$C/B$$

We deduced previously that the dividend of this expression is decreasing, and that the divisor is stable, why, so the new ratio will also have a downward trend in time. If we now simplify B in dividend and divisor this will not alter the outcome. Therefore the tendency of the remainder, i.e. A/C, is descending in the course of time.

In short, we have deduced that A/C is declining, which means that C grows more quickly than A, so **the production of consumer commodities tends to rise more rapidly than consumption of the same**. Putting it in other words, there is a natural tendency to overproduction of consumer commodities, and not all the produced commodities will find consumers on the market. This fact will have one of two consequences:

• With the passage of time there will be a crisis of overproduction; is it debatable whether it is a type of under consumption, or rather of disproportionality, in this case mismatch between production and consumption, but the trend is undeniable. We had already expressed previously that the causes of different types of crisis actually overlap each other, and that real crises often have a hybrid character.

Or

• We will have to drop one of the hidden assumptions according to which all generated productive capacity is put to work permanently. Indeed, if a part (in fact increased) of the means of production remain inactive in a more or less permanent basis, consumption and production of consumer commodities will remain in equilibrium, rather than unstable.

The second explanation corresponds with reality: the underuse of commodities production, with installed capacity utilization rates that rarely exceed the 75/80 and which require the deactivation of production means that have become physically or technologically obsolete.

Conclusions

In this way we have concluded the study of different types of crises, mentioned by Marx in a sometimes dispersed form, without leaving a true complete crisis theory. We have excluded as a central causal those arising from the rise of the organic composition of capital. We have kept as a valid explanation the fall of the rate of profit by wage growth, which would account, at least partially, for crises that occur after a period of expansive boom.

The mechanism described in this chapter is equally convincing to explain whether a crisis or the underemployment of installed capacity (in reality, despite all discussions of Marxism theoreticians, the underemployment and overproduction crises are two faces of the same coin), and finally we found that different imbalances can lead to crisis, although its nature is sporadic. There is no unique and unchanging cause of crises, but all listed factors collaborate in varying degrees in their generation. Marx has the merit of having developed a core of ideas at an early stage of development of the crises studies.

CHAPTER 10

Theory of the collapse

Forecasts on the collapse

Marx always had the certainty that the capitalist system is not eternal, and that it inevitably would be replaced by socialism. This would happen in a context in which capitalism would cease being a promoter of the development of the potential of humanity and become a chain or a pair of shackles that would delay or prevent that development. At that time, the working masses would shake this yoke to be released from the oppression and retardation factor.

However the author never exhibited a consistent theory of the way or the time in which that process would occur. Although Marx linked it somehow with the crises, he never delved in the mechanisms that would eventually trigger it.

His followers tried to fill that conceptual void and produced many divergent theories about the relationship between crisis and disappearance of the system, in the midst of general convulsions that would put an end to it.

Bernstein, Kautsky, Louis Boudin, Rosa Luxemburg and others issued predictions about such a process, but they were never accepted by the whole of the Marxist intellectuals, as were the descriptions of the types of crises, with all the limitations that we have discussed in the four preceding chapters. Therefore we cannot advance on the subject in a theoretical form due to lack of a concrete framework of ideas, in spite of the fact that the breakdown or collapse of the capitalist system was at all times an expectation of Marx and his followers.

What happened historically in this regard? The capitalist system as a whole has not fallen. The collapse that started in Russia in 1917 and continued throughout Eastern Europe after the World War II turned out to be reversible against all forecast, and the causes of the lengthy interruption of the system were rather related to the disastrous course of the first world war to the Czarist Russian Empire, and with the fall of Nazism and the presence of the Red Army after the end of war in Poland, the former Czechoslovakia, Bulgaria, Romania, the former East Germany, etc. This was in fact in agreement with the forecasts of Rosa Luxemburg, who had predicted that the wars and revolutions would bring the end of the system before the economic crisis reached its peak.

At the end of a period of up to seven decades in the case of the former Soviet Union, the Communist bloc fell, not by defeat or hazards on the war front, but because it could not face economic competition with the capitalist West.

What should be really frustrating to Marxists is the deep reason of the end of the Socialist experience in Eastern Europe: socialism had turned a heavy chain to the material progress of populations, which preferred to bear the painful transit back to capitalism rather than continuing with a gray reality and without a more promising future. That is, the reason why Marx hoped the departure of capitalism and entry to socialism was reversed in reality.

China came into the communism after World War II and crossed through the Cultural Revolution and the actions of the Red Guards the more radical and painful experience in the pursuit of change to human beings and delete all link to the past of their spirits and minds. Although today remains the political dominance of the Chinese Communist Party, it is very doubtful that we can qualify its economic system as pure communism, as it really was in the past. Indeed, after the Cultural Revolution they had to allow the return of partially capitalist structures in broad sections of the economy, process that is still going on at present.

In short, the end of capitalism as a result of a comprehensive crisis affecting most of humanity does not seem a realistic scenario today.

Depression

As said before Marx and his followers were always convinced that sooner or later the end of capitalism would occur, i.e. A point would be reached at which capitalism would no longer be possible because its economic decline would trigger the reaction of the masses eager to eliminate not only the injustice, but the corset that suffocated them. We have discussed the possibilities of a collapse and noticed that at present it seems not imminent. In the four centuries since the dawn of the system, capitalism has gone through periodic crises of different magnitude, but has continued to expand at a remarkable speed throughout the planet. The issue of the system unexpected survival has intrigued the followers of Marx, who began to attribute the survival of capitalism to the factors that act in the sense of moderating some of the prevailing trends in it, in particular the central and undisputed tendency to overproduction due to the higher speed of the growth of the production of consumer commodities compared to the growth of the actual effective consumption, according to what we have seen in the previous chapters. What interested them was to determine if these compensating factors, to which they attributed the survival, acted always with the same intensity, or if it could be expected that they would weaken with the passage of time, squarely facing the capitalist system with its internal contradictions. This would allow them to predict that in the absence of a sudden collapse of the system, at least could be expected its entry into a period of depression, that would eventually lead to turn anyway into a chain or shackles that would restrict the advancement of humanity and that they foretell its disappearance. The analysis turned then to those factors that counterbalanced the tendency to overproduction by the mentioned cause.

Marx had already prevented about the existence of such factors, although it is undeniable that he had not anticipated their strength and durability.

How do these factors work? Factors limiting the expansion of the production of consumer commodities above its demand and thus help preventing   crisis, should result in the following:

1. Growth of demand beyond expected levels: for example through the incorporation of new consumers previously marginalized, expansion of a credit system to consumption, execution of unproductive expenses that do not satisfy any need, growth of expenses of State and arms races, wars, etc.

2. Limitation of the growth of production of both consumer's commodities and production goods in such a way that they will not exceed the rate of growth of consumption: e.g. diversion of investment to new industries and products, failed investments, etc.

The Marxist intellectuals turned their attention to the development of these conditions, to forecast their future development. We will now explore these possible factors that have prevented the depression, with a view to determine if it can be expected they will continue acting in the future with the same or similar intensity that have done so to date, or if they can be expected to weaken or strengthen.

Factors limiting the growth of the production

• New industries: the way in which the emergence of new industries tends to eliminate or delay the growth of production, both of production goods and consumption commodities, beyond the possibilities of absorbing it, is related to the prolonged time which elapses between the start of the investment in fixed assets (factories, machinery, infrastructure) and the time in which production of new assets is taking place in full strength. Moreover, in the early days of those new industries the market has not yet acquired its definitive dimension and there is often unmet demand, exactly the opposite of the overproduction. Eventually investments mature, production rises rapidly to meet the demand, and a cycle of overproduction can happen. However, during that time the potential for crisis or depression was avoided. Mid-

20th-century Marxists watched with interest and hope this cause, and argued that the proportion of new industries on the total number of installed productive facilities was in a clear decrease because the main industries already existed (they mentioned in this respect industries from the Industrial Revolution, such as steel, automotive, textiles, railways, machine tools, etc. The general impression was that all that could be imagined in terms of industry already existed, and the conclusion that emanated from this analysis was that new industries as factors that delayed the crisis of overproduction tended to disappear. Half a century later it is difficult to share this opinion; the enormous range of industries and new products that have emerged in the meantime and are emerging daily suggest rather the opposite conclusion, particularly based on the very high speed of emergence of entirely new and unsuspected sectors. Decidedly, this expectation of crisis should be entirely discarded at least for the moment.

• Failed investments: as expressed above, employers do not have complete information about the markets in which they operate, and thus cannot fully anticipate the result of their endeavors. This is particularly true in the case of new products, new niche markets, novice entrepreneurs or territorial areas. For this reason often the businessmen make wrong decisions, incorrectly sized or untimely that lead to the failure of their attempts, and lead them to prolonged periods of poor results or directly to bankruptcy, rendering fruitless the investments made and assets acquired, which abandon production, limiting in this way the growth of production above consumption and tendency to overproduction crises. The Marxist authors have realized that with greater statistical information, marketing techniques and the work of consultants of all kinds, this factor limiting the crisis is losing importance, what is an alternative way of saying that investments are generally more productive than in the past and therefore the brake to overproduction is weakening. It is possible that this trend is true, and what is a lucky event for some individual capitalists may bring some adverse consequences for the system as a whole. Anyway, this is hardly a causal for global crises or extended depression, or therefore a pre-announcement of the end of the capitalist system.

Factors that increase the pace of consumption

• Population growth: first, it should be clarified that what really matters is the growth of the labor force that is the mass of population effectively incorporated into labor and consumer markets. This can occur for two reasons: i) absolute population growth, ii) incorporation into these markets of population previously excluded due to geographical, cultural, transport, etc reasons. The importance of this clarification will become obvious when we look at the current and future prospects for this cause of crisis or depression.

We had deduced mathematically and repeatedly explained that the main reason for the crisis by overproduction lies in the commodities production growth above the actual speed of consumption. In this context the increase of solvent population - i.e. that is the people that have means to finance their consumption, eliminates or delays that trend and allows the system to run with high rates of accumulation without dangers of overproduction.

An additional and intuitive explanation is obtained reasoning that the population growth allows to expand the variable capital (contract workers) without reducing the reserve army - i.e. the rate of unemployment - which helps to keep wage rises below its value, and therefore maintain the rate of surplus value.

Should the rate of growth of the population (and of the labor force) descend, wage pressures will increase simply because of the law of supply and demand, and as a result the efforts of the capitalists by replacing variable capital by constant capital- i.e. men by machines- will be increased. If consumer base is reduced there is no lock that prevents that the production will increase more rapidly than consumption, and the possibility of crisis or depression will grow.

There is thus an inverse relationship between population growth and the tendency to overproduction (or under-consumption).

Are there any defined trends in the field of population growth? This book is not the place to develop demographic analysis, but we will remember what was said above that what really counts is the population linked to production and consumption, a concept similar to that of "economically active population". Despite the rise in unemployment in several Western countries, huge masses have been and are still being incorporated each year in China, India and Southeast Asia and this globally compensates such vacancy. There is no doubt that globally, the employed population is in a process of significant growth. Looking ahead, there are still hundreds of millions of people in those same countries yet to enter the markets, and is reasonable to expect that this process will continue with the rest of Asia and Africa and some countries in Latin America. It does not seem as the counterweight of the crisis of overproduction will be exhausted soon although in some countries the local situation is different, because of the migration of jobs to cheap labor countries.

• Unproductive consumption: with this name Marx and his successors referred to the consumption of which they improperly called unproductive classes. They had placed that name thinking in landlords, nobles and members of the clergy, members of servitude, *lumpen proletariat* or marginal elements, and in the end other sectors not related to the production process and not included in the variable capital and surplus value, i.e. all those who were neither capitalists nor workers. These sectors however had their means of life, and somehow their income was deducted of surplus value to provide for their consumption, so these resources are removed from the accumulation, and therefore help to prevent the phenomenon of overproduction, since on the one hand they reduce the productive investment and on the other they increase the total consumption. Over time, and always maintaining the definition of unproductive consumption, the heirs of Marx were adding large groups to these classes, including vendors and ultimately all persons linked to distribution channels, the professionals, teachers and professors and the vast majority of the members of the middle class, of strong expansion in the 20th century and so far in the 21st. Curiously they continued to hold the thesis of Marx, in the sense that the evolution of this unproductive consumption thus defined was decreasing, so the its importance as a factor counteracting the tendency to overproduction or under consumption would diminish in time, what would ensure the end of capitalism by crisis or depression. This thesis is in clear contrast with the trends observable in the almost all of the societies. Classes that are not directly related to the circuit of industrial production have grown much more than the capitalists and workers in number, importance and volume of consumption, and extended beyond the manufacturing workers in post-industrial societies. Today it would be unthinkable to call them "unproductive classes" as they hold positions of enormous importance and recognition in modern communities. The evolution of this factor opposing overproduction is clearly increasing permanently.

• State expenditures: this factor should be included within the former, since at the time and in the vision of Marx it included basically the expenditures of royalty, their entourages, military, judges and some other sectors that fit the definition of unproductive classes. However, because of its size and importance, it is preferable to give to the State, particularly to the modern State, a treatment apart. Since Marx wrote Capital, the State, even in capitalist countries, has grown in size, functions and importance in society and therefore also in consumption, becoming usually one of the largest global consumers. Following some authors- both Marxists and non-Marxists- we will divide State spending in three major areas:

State spending and capital investment : it includes all wages, raw material and other expenses in the activities of the State in the role of production of commodities and services for sale, including public services, such as water, power, gas, transport etc. in which the State impersonates functions that are carried out by the private sector in many other countries. In these cases, State-owned enterprises obtain a profit that is reinvested, so the way this process is configured is completely indistinguishable from the private accumulation. From the point of view that concerns us, these types of expenses do not constitute a factor counteracting the tendency to overproduction, so it should be excluded from the analysis.

2. Transfers of the State: This concept includes payments that the State performs and is not connected to the rented provision of commodities and services. They include important figures in respect of retirement and pensions where they are in charge of the State, subsidies of any kind, interests of public debt, etc. The role of these transfers in the reduction of overproduction which concerns us is given by the source and destination of the funds that comprise it. If the source has been from taxes on employment, or drawdown of the wage they will tend to aggravate the under consumption, while if they have been imposed to the capitalists income or equity they will subtract funds to the accumulation process. To complete the analysis we must consider the destination of these payments: retirements and pensions go directly to expand consumption; interests to expand corporate income and normally they will be reinserted to the accumulation process, subsidies to consumers will counteract the overproduction and subsidies to producers will increase it. We can say that in a normal economy the general trend of State transfers should be to increase consumption with resources partially removed from the accumulation process. It is what is commonly called redistribution of income.

3. Consumption of State: Expenses of the Executive, legislative and judicial branches, military functions, etc. The amount of these expenses is usually very important. With regard to its function in our topic, what was said in the previous paragraph holds valid: depends on whether the funds were obtained subtracting them of wages or from surplus value and thus from business profits. All the money that enters the state consumption comes from private consumption (in which case it is neutral to the subject overproduction), or detracts from accumulation. In the second case it is a powerful factor to curb overproduction crises.

Besides the three types of State expenditures mentioned, there are other ways in which it can influence not only the economy but the propensity to overproduction we are studying. On one side the State can generate inflation through its various monetary, fiscal, labor, etc. policies. The effect of inflation through monetary creation has the effect of increasing consumption, although this effect may be partially neutralized since increased government spending may be accompanied by the decrease in the purchasing power of the population. Anyway its net effect is normally pro- consumption. Loans granted to government agencies to finance expenditures and investments can dislodge (crowding out) private bank credit to population, in which case the effect will depend on whether it is the running costs of consumption or the productive investment outlays that predominate within State expenditure, and whether the dislodged are mostly private companies that no longer have access to credit for production, or workers who want to finance their consumption.

Finally, since the global crisis of 1930 anti-cyclical policies have widely spread in many countries generally tending to reduce expenditure in times of economic boom and expand it in times of recession. The effects of these measures are to increase or decrease consumption and therefore aggravate or improve the trend to under consumption, according to what we have previously seen.

But what is really important is to highlight that the modern State has and uses powerful tools that can balance the tendency to overproduction or under consumption as defined by Marx and his followers.

Conclusion

From all the extensive treatment that we have made on the factors that counteract the tendency to depression or crisis by overproduction and its current and future evolution emerges clearly that none of them gives symptom of fatigue or is expected to lose strength in the future. Capitalism, from the point of view of Marxist analysis, has reinsurance, which is a dubious blessing from the point of view of the system, in particular with regard to the growth of unproductive consumption and the active role of the State that was explained in the previous paragraph.

In all this analysis, there is an issue that draws attention: all factors counteracting the process of accumulation and in particular that decreases the reinvestment of past earnings turn to be positive because it slows down the tendency to overproduction. This is in flagrant contradiction with all the economic theory that fosters the convenience of high rates of saving in the economy, and the subsequent productive investment as a basis for sustainable growth. The contrast that takes place among the economies of East Asia, which are praised for their very high rates of savings-investment, with Latin America's lowest savings in relation to gross domestic product is a classical example on how investment is considered.

Alternative theories about the capitalist crises:

There have been other explanations about the origin and development of the crisis of the capitalist system, and some of them do not come from the heart of Marxism. Although the theme of this book is the political economy of Marx, it is not idle try to briefly expose an alternative point of view, to put in relief what is specifically Marxist

We have selected the case of the theories of Joseph Alois Schumpeter, an Austrian economist, author of a theory of economic cycles, context in which he deals with crisis. We will do a schematic presentation of his ideas.

Schumpeter departs of a "theory of innovation", which is understood as a sudden and radical change of the production function. The trigger for innovation may be of a technological nature, or the discovery of new ways of producing or transporting commodities, opening of new markets, access to new sources of raw material, or major alterations in industrial organization. The entrepreneur has the central role, which may or may not be the inventor or owner of the patent for the purpose of innovation and may or may not be the owner of capital that is invested. His basic role is leadership, organizing around his project an economic space where innovation plays its role. This character usually starts acting in the declining phase of a previous economic cycle, during which tunes the object of its innovation, usually with much effort. At a certain point the circumstances begin to change, and entrepreneurs emerge in clusters around the pioneers, while an ascending phase begins to emerge. New companies based on innovation begin to appear and grow, which will be dislodging the old leaders of their positions, heading to the decline and disappearance. The process of capitalist investment develops at the beginning with setbacks, while the overall economy regroups and takes momentum. The launch of the new wave does not start from at end point of the previous cycle, so that many of the previous players will not be part of the new game. Then the system grows rapidly, driving from depression to boom which however carries the seeds of the new downward phase of the cycle and eventually depression in her womb. Crises are a result of periods of rise and vice versa.

The result of the process is what Schumpeter called "creative destruction", where the new economy wipes out the old structures eliminating a large proportion of outdated production capacity.

In short, to Schumpeter-who however was pessimistic about the future of capitalism - crises are not the prelude to the collapse of the system, but the normal form of capitalist development, through successive business cycles.

THIRD PART

The big issues

The following chapters will be the Marxian classics, concerning the role of the State, the dynamics of capitalism including its specific accumulation process, the formation of monopolies, the international economy, the construction of the socialism, criticism of the reformist path, the theoretical base of historical materialism in which is based political economy Marx, and the legacy that the theoretical and practical development of a century and a half of Marxist socialism left to present and future generations.

CHAPTER 11

The role of the State

The classical and in general all non-Marxists economists visualize the economy as a science that investigates in particular the relations of production and distribution within the broader scope of the interactions between man and nature, by which the State does not constitute the primary focus of study, although it is considered t at the time of analyzing how are shaped the mentioned relations, but rather as an external factor which constrains them and configure them.

Marx and his successors criticized this definition arguing that it emphasizes the character of natural and inevitable of such relationships, what prevent understanding their contingent and transitory nature. He then defined Economy as the science that studies the social production relations under certain historically conditions. The essential difference is that relations of production are not seen as belonging to the realm of nature but as a product of certain historical preconditions that led to their realization.

Consistent with their definition of Economy, non Marxists authors described the State as an institution that acts in the interests of the whole society, mediating and reconciling diverging interests that arise naturally in it, in order to provide solutions that are acceptable for all competing sectors. In particular, it acts in conflicts between the social classes trying to harmonize the crossed interests.

As was the case with crises, Marx never developed a complete theory on the role of the State, but in his writings and those of his successors there is enough material that allows knowing their thinking in detail.

First, they question the unchangeable character of the class structure of capitalism in the light of historical knowledge that accounts for the succession of arrangements that different societies have had. On the basis of this assertion Marx wonders what has been the role of the State in the maintenance of the existing social structure, and came to the conclusion that it is the guarantor of the continuity of that structure. The State is thus the institution which monopolizes the use of force in order to sustain over time the social relations and in particular the property relations in which all the rest are based. In other words, there is a close correlation between the functions of the State and bourgeois property relations. The protection of property relations is, according to Marxist theory, the imposition of the domination of classes. Summarizing, Marxists propose, as opposed to the Liberal theory of mediation between classes, a theory of class domination. It is interesting to note that the disciples of Marx distinguished between private ownership in simple reproduction, where every craftsman had his work utensils, and capitalist private property, which is based not so much in the possession of things, but in social relations, relations between people, some of whom may have the fruit of the work of others by the fact that they hold possession of the means of production.

Therefore, in the Communist Manifesto Marx and Engels summarized their objective in this regard: "Abolition of private property". For everything said above, this goal cannot be achieved without a confrontation with the bourgeois state.

The economic role of the State

As expressed above, the Marxian analysis of the role of the State focused almost exclusively on what Marx and his followers defined as its fundamental task: to protect the subsistence of capitalism and private property, in particular of the forces seeking to subvert them, basically the Communists. In this way, they made reference to the "Police State " functions, paying little attention to the increased and numerous functions that the modern State, with large differences from country to country, takes over in the economic and social areas. Indeed, the analysis of the economic functions of the State is an unfinished task of Marxism. Anyway, the modern communist intellectuals admit that the State carries out tasks with strong impact on the economy. Starting with the discussions on limitation of the workday in England social legislation has continued to increase throughout the world, which is in contrast with the role assigned by Marx. This has led his followers to give an interpretation on this apparent anomaly, which can be summarized in the following way:

• The primary role of the bourgeois state is, as expressed above, the preservation of the continuity and stability of capitalism and its order.

• This does not preclude in certain circumstances that legislation is approved that puts concrete limits to class exploitation, as in the case of labor laws. The purpose thereof is to placate of class antagonisms before they give origin to revolutionary uprisings.

• It cannot be expected that the sum of the concessions made to the working class will change the essence of the capitalist system. With this they antagonize to Social democrats and other reformists who hoped to introduce sufficient changes to the system to make disappear the exploitation of man by man, at least in its most degrading aspects.

This late addition to the alleged fundamental purpose of the State falls short in its scope. It does not include essential tasks of the State with direct impact on economic activity, such as the development of infrastructure (routes, energy, communications, transport etc.), promoting scientific development and technological on which most industries and other modern economic activities are based, the defense of the productive activities of each country in the international arena, vocational and technical education, the delimitation of the professional duties where it does not involve conflicts between classes, etc. The functions of the State in primarily non-economic areas but with a decisive influence on the economic development of a society, such as general education, health, security, foreign relations, environmental sanitation and many others are not mentioned either.

One wonders if this disdain for the study of the State is because, at the time Marx was writing the general guidelines, the existing States did not fully perform these functions. Or else he realized that taking them into account would approach the definition of the role of the State in the liberal version of mediation and conciliation of different interests existing in the society, and above all it would implicitly recognize that even in the bourgeois society there is a common good for all its members.

On the other hand, if it is true that numerous reforms in more than one century they have not changed the relations of property of the capitalist system, it is also true that the effect of such changes has been fundamental not in abstract notions but in the concrete living conditions of a large and growing portion of humanity. Criticism of the reformists should be judged in the light of the concrete and lasting achievements obtained by them compared to all countries that were or are ruled by the Communists.

The theme of political democracy

Marxists have always considered political democracy in a way that is at least ambiguous. They have demanded democracy in the midst of authoritarian governments, but not by real conviction of the superiority of such a system, but only because sectors that advocate communism find greater possibilities to operate and to make their claims and actions in democracy. In other words, their commitment to democracy is instrumental and provisional.

For that reason they criticize the Democratic Socialists, who rely on democracy to get the power and change the current capitalist society to another Socialist through a series of gradual and incremental reforms. Marxists argue, perhaps rightly, that the possible changes from the inside of bourgeois society are precisely within the boundaries of this kind of society. Therefore they do not have too many hopes in democracy, and in reality their commitment to it is only tactical.

In fact, Marx may not be accused of having democratic deviations. He always trumpeted the *dictatorship of the proletariat* to carry humanity to socialism and assign for "violence the role of midwife of History".

Actually, in his time the democratic countries were a handful in all the Earth and nothing permitted foreseeing that the democratic system, even in its external expressions, was going to grow in the face of the planet. In relation to his followers, the typical Marxist-Leninist method to take power in general was not based in free elections in which they could get majority of votes, but in the actions of politicized elites and an allegedly enlightened minority, which took advantage of violent revolutions where social demands were mixed with anti-colonial struggles, global wars, patriotism and other considerations which gave a broader scope to the demands of these minorities, and provided them with a social support that would have been impossible to get only their own flags and programs. Once in power, democracy was never established by the Communists. It is simply that the gene of democracy does not exist in the Marxist DNA.

CHAPTER 12

Concentration of Capital

The analysis performed above on the structure of capitalism departs from a concept that was not made explicit at the time: the existence of free competition in the economies concerned, i.e. that there are no barriers to the entry of new competitors in each of the major markets, and all bidders play with the same rules and have the same opportunities for doing business. To express it in Marxist terms, we have proceeded in a relatively high abstraction level in this aspect. The real world not always follows this course, which has given rise- both in the Marxist and non-Marxist bibliographies- to the study of imperfect competition and monopolies in its different variants (duopolies, oligopolies).

The source of this tendency towards the concentration of capital in the terminology of Marx lies in the organic composition of capital already defined in previous chapters, and certain movements in the interior of this composition.

Indeed with the accumulation process, we have seen that it expands the proportion of the constant capital (consisting of machinery, buildings, facilities, raw materials and other materials) to the variable capital (labor). But in addition also is expanded within the constant capital the proportion invested in machinery, buildings and installations (fixed assets in accounting terminology) against the part represented by raw materials and materials. All this produces a scale change in industrial establishments in favor of dimensions increasingly larger belonging to firms becoming more and more concentrated. They have economies of scale that allow them to lower their costs and sell more cheaply, leaving out competition rivals with smaller size and particularly of lower financial capability, preventing them from investing to match these economies of scale.

Centralization of capital

As just stated, the accumulation and concentration of capital enlarge the scale of production by continuous reinvestment of surplus value from that permits creating new production assets. Besides the concentration already discussed, Marx distinguishes a process called centralization of capital that has some distinctive characteristics with respect to the former. It is the unification of existing capital, either because some the previous holders were left out of action by competitive financially stronger rivals, or voluntary capital addition in larger units, a process that in this case does not deprive previous capital owners of their ownership of part of the enlarged companies, but removes companies in the competitive struggle. What characterizes this process of centralization according to Marx is not so much the unification in the ownership of the capital, as the unified management of large companies.

A paragraph apart deserves what Marx calls credit system, which includes banks and financial entities of investment of all types, system that favors and lubricates the process of centralization, sucking funds of the society and making it available for bigger and more solid capitalists. Thus, the creation of stock societies of different character allowed increase in an extraordinary degree the size of most powerful companies, to the point of allowing them to undertake ventures that other way would not have been possible. Marx offers as an example the construction of railways, which would have been impossible for individual capitalists, no matter how large they were.

The process of centralization, studied by Marx and his successors, has three main consequences:

• Increasing the size of the companies in prodigious proportions it prevents that these can be managed by the usual methods, favoring the implementation of scientific and rational methods of direction. Marx hoped that this process would pave the way for the direction of Socialist enterprises of the future.

• Centralization is both product and cause of the incorporation of technology to companies, so that the automation process feeds back, eliminating labor on the way.

• Tends to suppress competition and encourage monopoly favoring the creation of huge conglomerates. This fact was suggested Marx not only the trend was in the sense not only of leaving on foot a single company by branch of activity, but to consolidate companies acting in the various branches of the industry under a unified leadership.

Corporations

Appearance of corporations in the scene was studied carefully by Marx and his followers. In addition to the enormous expansion of scale of action which we have mentioned above, he distinguished other phenomena derived from its inception.

In the first place, even within the limits of capitalism, corporations represent somehow the transformation of a capitalist private ownership in social ownership that is property of a set of individuals, with the consequences that this brings in the limitation of the exercise of the will of each one of the capitalists. Besides, the figure of the capitalist-owner and concurrently director of his company splits in two different characters. On the one hand the owner of capital "released" from his executive duties at the head of the company and who is fully dedicated to enjoy his property, and on the other the manager or professional director, who makes decisions every day on behalf of the funds owners. This is part of the streamlining of the business direction and its foundation in scientific principles which Marx had foreseen as a prelude of the socialism, and that we have mentioned above. We must add however that the range of decisions of professional managers is restricted to actions and tactical ones, as we shall see below, since the major strategic decisions are in other hands.

With the emergence of stock enterprises and capital markets a new phenomenon occurs: the owner of the capital has a site where can get rid of his property and get reunited with its liquid capital for reinvestment elsewhere, without further consideration or worries about the fate of the former company. This fact had huge consequences on the companies in the economic, social and even psychological fields. The shareholder happens to be closer to the lender that gives access to its money to the Corporation on a temporary basis, which to be to compensated for being exposed to losses will require a higher rate of return Another important figure who the followers of Marx analyzed is that called "promoter", who throws new developments at the capital markets, usually receive great benefits by that initial task. This function was absorbed by big trade banks in Europe and by the so-called investment banks in the United States.

Due to all these facts Marx´s followers assumed that the system would be governed thereafter entirely by what they called "financial capital", extrapolating in excessive tendencies that are evidenced and are still evident.

There is still an additional phenomenon and important consequence of the massive emergence of corporations. Since the possession of shares are normally dispersed among a large number of stockholders, in order to take control of these large units and running them it is unnecessary to own or to represent the total and not even the majority of the shares. For the really big companies the percentage of control is usually between the third and the fourth part of the stock. The holders of these packages can decide about the destinations of the total of the company, increasing its degree of control to entities much larger than their own capital amounts.

In addition, with the stock cross linking and other corporate combinations, one specific company can take control of another company, whereupon the first control group extended its sphere of action to both firms, in a process that can be repeated countless times. Although in this case there is no disempowerment of the rest of the shareholders of the companies involved, and they continue to claim their dividends, they do not really have access to its direction, and delegate all the responsibility to the parent group. These groups have often been described as a "financial aristocracy", which actually would have in their hands the fate of these giants.

Monopolistic combinations

A further stage in the restriction of competition is the combinations of different types between companies operating in the same market.

With increasing size as was described in the previous paragraphs, larger firms with larger financial capacity get economies of scale and therefore decrease in costs that enable them to sell at lower prices, which lead to widespread reductions in the profit rates, bringing often many competitors into bankruptcy. Therefore the survivors begin talks to avoid the cutthroat competition and stabilize markets and prices. The agreements cover an assortment of modalities that range from the informal to the formal, starting with the so-called gentlemen's agreements that tend to be bounded in time and of limited scope. The so-called pools usually involve price agreements and market and production shares for each of the participants. Cartels and trusts are formalized, and in the latter case is often constituted a board of trustees which takes in charge the direction of the so-formed combination. Finally the mergers involve the disappearance of previous legal entities and the emergence of a new larger company.

Most countries adopted in the first half of the XX century anti-trust legislation in order to preserve competition in the markets and protect consumers from abuses and the greed of cartels; the trusts were normally forbidden, and conditions were set to functions that involve the obligation of companies that are reorganizing in this way to divest certain assets to avoid the reduction of the number of bidders in a certain market. The real effects of these laws has been to slow down the process of concentration, but failed to prevent it completely. World markets in many of industries have undergone very marked processes of concentration, leaving a few competitors at global level in certain cases. Even formerly very fragmented industries like the pharmaceutical are today much more centralized to a few decades ago.

Marx did not live this stage of business combinations, his friend Friedrich Engels came to incorporate some notes regarding them when he collecting the third volume of Capital from the notes left by Marx.

These themes were taken up by economic authors of all trends, and actually the most important discrepancies relate to the meaning they have for the future of the capitalist system. The action of monopolies was not only the object of attention from economists and political parties; consumer associations and other NGOs (non-governmental organizations have denounced and fought the monopolistic practices in different countries

Financial capital

We have already mentioned that banks played an important role in the process that led to the concentration of capital and the reduction in competition, but it is interesting to follow the evolution that role has had in the course of the last century and a half.

For their outstanding role in the issue of shares of large companies and the provision of funds to finance the growth of the largest firms in each branch, banks appeared associated with all processes of cartelization of the XIX and beginning of the XX century. Industrial enterprises had to share decision-

137

making with bankers who made their funds available to the former so they could crystallize their investment projects in new assets and purchase of companies and mergers between them, which are very capital demanding processes. Some Marxist authors, including Hilferding, extrapolated this trend to infinity, predicting that eventually there would be one surviving firm in every branch of industry, and that the banks would dominate them completely, becoming the true global central power. This led to a very intense controversy within communism in which intervened even Lenin, relativizing the most extreme positions.

The further development of events followed a different path to that foreseen by Hilferding. After the first wave of concentration, industrial enterprises began to fund their further expansion with funds generated from their own businesses, retained profits- i.e. that were not distributed to shareholders as dividends- and especially with the huge funds represented by the depreciation of fixed assets and depreciation, which from the accounting point of view do not constitute profits but is money that remains in the equity of the companies for their use. Self-generated capital was taking the central role in the funding of companies moving banks to a subsidiary but still important role as providers of industrial capital. On the other hand, although centralization continued, it never produced the extreme concentration in one firm in each branch, but usually the process stops when there are several companies competing to each other, each of them with an important participation in the market. Going further in the process of concentration would be dysfunctional, as eliminating one of those giant competitors would represent costs far higher than any monopoly benefits that it would arise.

In recent decades, in their desire to get rid of the dependence of the banks, huge firms that have been involved in mergers and acquisitions, exceeding their capacity of self-financing, have attended directly capital markets not through commercial banks - that lend their own funds, deposited in them by their customers - but rather through the so-called investment banks, which do not provide their own funds but help vacuuming them from the public through stock exchanges. This has forced large industrial groups to make major changes to their entrepreneur profile, to suit the palate of the investors frequently guided by risk evaluating companies and gurus of all kinds. It was thus that we have witnessed the dismantling of large conglomerates including chemical, pharmaceutical, agrochemical etc. divisions and giving rise to still larger companies but more homogeneous in terms of their investment portfolio. In the same way, although for different reasons, commercial banks were forced in some countries to separate their equities from investment banks, to avoid cross-contamination risks, in particular for the accounts of commercial banks.

Although Marx did not live to participate in these discussions, it was considered interesting to treat them briefly, since the role of financial capital is under permanent discussion in all countries of the world, including the central economies

The failure of predictions on the extreme centralization of capital in just one concurrent handled by a single bank show the limitations of the extrapolations made at particular moments of economic history, after which conditions change profoundly due to the influence of circumstances which did not exist or had been ignored for not being at the level of abstraction (using the Marxist terminology) used by the theorist. The problem is that the very concept of abstraction levels, leaving aside factors that do not seem relevant at a historic moment, produces sometimes very rigid models based on them, especially when the neglected factors take a much bigger dimension and shape the new reality.

CHAPTER 13

Monopolies

We have already seen in the previous chapter the causes that act in the capitalist societies leading eventually to the formation of monopolies. We will now explore their effects.

Marx explains that in markets dominated by monopolies prices and quantities of production are limited by the purchasing power and the desires of consumers, without reference to the costs and value of the commodities, as they arise from the theory of the value. So we cannot expect here that actual selling prices will tend to converge the value of the goods that is the amount of money determined by the average social work content to make that good. In other words, the theory of value is invalid here. In the absence of competition, monopolistic companies fix their selling prices at the highest possible level compatible with the possibilities for consumers to pay them. In general, prices of monopoly markets are thus higher than in competitive markets, and the quantities produced are lower. The possibility of monopolistic suppliers to raise their prices is limited only by the so-called price-elasticity of the product. IN other words, it limited by the possibility of consumers to dispense with the product or to replace it with another good. In the case of inelastic products buyers are completely in hands of monopolies. Authors of all political trends are in agreement with all this.

Monopolistic profit rates are logically higher than those of companies working in conditions of competition, thus fulfilling the ultimate goal of the monopolistic action. Now, since in fact the value of the total output of society is not increased, such actions constitute a zero-sum game, and extra surplus value obtained by monopolies is extracted from the rest of society; that is from the total mass of wages (variable capital) of workers, and from the surplus value of the rest of the capitalists that they do not enjoy conditions of monopoly. How much is removed each of these two sources depends on the bargaining power of labor unions. If this is high, the profits of other capitalists will suffer to a greater extent. In this way, the whole society is harmed by the presence in their midst of monopolistic markets; that explains the strong support antitrust laws and action receive in many countries.

As the remaining entrepreneurs lack the possibility of fixing monopoly overcharges to their products, the trend towards equalization of rates of profit mentioned in previous chapters is without effect also here. This trend will continue however acting in those markets that remain competitive. The tendency of capital to migrate to areas of higher profit rates, also explained before, is hampered in the case of the access to monopolistic markets by effective barriers to entry, whether these are of legal nature, technology, due to the exclusivity of certain raw materials, patents, access to very large sources of funding, etc. In general, a situation close to perfect competition works where technologies are available to all competitors, production scales are small or medium-sized, access to credit is broad, there are no obstacles of legal or other type at the entrance of producers, products are commodities, i.e. products more or less standardized, composition and manufacture are very similar and are produced by a multitude of suppliers, none of which is a determining factor in prices; in this case manufacturers are price takers in the market.

Monopolies and accumulation

Monopolies have a profound influence on the process of accumulation in the environment in which they operate. In general, the more concentrated is the capital in such medium, the greater the proportion of it that will accumulate. This has to do with the increase in the surplus value and profit rates that monopolies produce, allowing firms to allocate more to reinvestment.

However, one of the conditions for the maintenance of monopoly is not to expand the production and offer of monopolized commodities, which could lead to the reduction of the price and the on profit. Ultimately, monopolies not only keep away potential competitors through the handling of the barriers to entry in their businesses, but it also limits their own reinvestment in the monopoly business, eliminating any probability of oversupply.

They are then forced to allocate the surplus of revenues to investments outside the monopoly category, even though the rate of profit is less in them than in their sphere of domain. What happens is that they must defend the extra profit of monopoly origin at any cost, so the smaller profits produced by investing in areas of less profitability is more than offset by the conservation of the aforementioned extra profit. Therefore they seek to maintain their market dominating position without shortages but also without surplus supply.

Using as explained the surplus accumulated capital to competitive markets that already have their offer satisfied by other competitors, monopolies will increase in them what the

Marxist authors consider is the risk of an overproduction or under consumption crisis, whose the scope we have however relativized in earlier chapters. Another conclusion of the disciples of Marx is that incorporation of technological innovations in the monopoly sectors is slower than that in other economic areas, and that they are generally focused in replacing labor by machines rather than expanding production scales.

Role of trade

The role of trade was treated by Marx in a rather circumstantial way and is not the brightest part of his theory. We have briefly mentioned within the subject of unproductive expenditure in previous chapters, and we will devote it broader paragraph in this context.

We have seen that the value of a commodity is determined according to Marx by the addition of the constant and variable parts of capital and of the surplus value expressed in the process of the commodity production: constant capital includes the raw material, the production equipment and the manufacturing plants, the variable capital incorporates the wages of productive labor, and surplus value is that pocketed by the industrial entrepreneur. Where do then the expenses incurred by the merchant and his profit in the process of bringing commodities to end users come from? Marx responds that they are detractions to the surplus value of the industrial entrepreneur, who then has his profit reduced, and by diluting it in a larger number of hands; the consequence is to lower the average profit rate of a society. All costs and profits from the commercial sector are sterile and the labor occupied by it and its consumption are equally unproductive. Somehow Marx separates the costs of transport and storage - what we would call today Logistics costs - and adds them to the costs of production and therefore the value of a good, even when they are incurred by the merchant, as frequently happens. But the costs of sales personnel, accounting, administrative, etc. and the profit of the merchant remain unproductive, and the sector as a whole has according to Marx a parasitical role. For that reason, when we discuss unproductive expenditure in the context of the crisis of overproduction, such character was assigned to trade employees, along with serfs, etc.

Ultimately, according to the Marxist analysis trade has three overall effects on the development of capitalism:

1) It increases the costs of the system, reducing the available total surplus value, which slows the process of accumulation.

(2) The profit is distributed among a larger number of business units, which reduces the average rate of profit. Above we explained that this in itself delays further accumulation.

(3) It increases consumption, adding a number of mouths that earn an income for their work.

All three factors, as we have seen in previous chapters, have an antagonistic effect on the emergence of overproduction or under consumption crisis.

Whatever the opinion on the categorization made by Marx on trade and those involved in it, it should be noted that maintaining the coherence of the Marxist scheme involves certain hard definitions. In the case of trade, this categorization is at least striking, since it was an ancient and important autonomous activity already in the time of Marx. Additionally one could think that the author could have expanded the notion of creating value to all those activities that are necessary to make sure that a good reaches its end users and adapt the economic scheme to this definition without major problems. But it is possible that this concept was not in the original Marxist DNA, and successors have not had the autonomy to modify the master option. One can also wonder if, along with the failure of central planning, this disdain for the distribution of the commodities is not at the base of the sad and endless queues of buyers in search of the life-essential assets that were the daily reality in the former grey Soviet Union and other countries of the Eastern Bloc.

Consequences

Marx followers described that once a certain degree of concentration in a particular industry, competition between the remaining monopolistic players - or rather oligopolistic- fighting ceases to be represented by successive prices drops to evict the others, and is replaced by advertising action and others linked to the trade and distribution channels, to which a parasitic character is assigned. This statement is at least doubtful, since attributing to advertising actions a monopolistic nature is a contradiction in terms. They actually are competitive alternative measures to lowering prices and they existed always, whether in monopolistic or competitive situations; the only change is the size of the companies that compete in this way, and the massive nature of the means by which these actions usually run,

With regard to the political consequences of this growth of the marketing and distribution areas Marx and his disciples lashed out at the incipient middle class, with much less political weight in his time than at present. It is made up of all kinds of professionals, technicians, bureaucrats of the State and the private sector, small business owners, and is actually fed back by employees of commercial, logistics, advertising, etc.

As Marx only admitted the surplus value created in the industrial sector, he did not conceive that businessmen are also extracting surplus value to the rest of the workers. For this reason, he judged that both capitalists and employees in these sectors (commercial, etc.) obtained their income subtracting it from the surplus value of the industrialists. This fact would create a community of interests between these employers and their employees, or at least reduced antagonism to the existing in the industrial sector. Consequently, the Marxist authors argue that the middle class will ally itself with the bourgeois and against proletarians in defense of capitalism and their livelihood, stemming from the rate of surplus value of the industrial sector. This conclusion provides u with a questionable explanation, fruit of the rigidity of previous basic definitions.

CHAPTER 14

Global economy

Marx defined the principles and laws of his political economy basically at a national level. International trade was already much extended in his time, but had not reached the levels of integration and universality that has today. The economies of the last half of the 19th century were basically national economies with overseas links of varied importance.

A key question is whether the law of value, as Marx defined it is still valid at the global level; in particular, it is relevant to ask whether commodities tend to exchange among themselves on the basis of the value calculated on the content of average social work time. We must remember that such premise is founded on the mobility of the labor force, which migrates from an industry to another for levels of compensation which may be obtained on them. Also, the capital is free to move from one production branch to another guided by the profit rates prevailing in them.

We anticipate that these premises are not met completely on an international scale.

In particular the international mobility of labor is far from being as smooth as within the confines of each country. There are numerous impediments to the massive flows of population, whether of legal type, for the costs of transportation and installation in a new environment, including economic, personal and psychological costs associated with intercultural clashes, a problem never easy to solve.

The movements of international capital, although not so exposed to avatars as human displacement, can also be problematic for tax and legal reasons, existence of protectionism, etc. But what ultimately prevents the action of the law of value to planetary scale is the low mobility of workers. According to most Marxists authors we can state a general rule as follows: the law of value acts only where there is a uniform and mobile work force, i.e., commodities tend to be interchanged depending on their average social work time only in those cases.

We cannot then expect that commodities traded internationally will be changed in proportion to their heterogeneous contents of working time.

As wage levels are dissimilar in different countries, we can expect that surplus value rates will be different, and if the only acting factor is trade, so will also be the profit rates. If concurrently with trade there is export of capital - in general there is a flow of capital from rich countries to the less developed ones - profit rates will tend to equalize, since funds that migrate from countries of high development and low profit rates to reach countries of higher profit rates, which gradually begin to descend as the most profitable investment opportunities are saturated,

The trend towards the international equalization of profit rates does not imply a similar trend to the equalization of surplus rates. These are due to different causes: profit rates are homogenized by the export of capital, which in general is fairly free of restrictions that may hinder it, since most of the countries are willing and even eager to receive capital from abroad. On the other hand, as we have said, there usually exist restrictions on the movements of people and therefore labor force, and by reason neither wages nor surplus value are equalized across countries.

As there is a formula that links all three values that we have deduced and used in previous chapters, we can now add that if the rate of profit tends to be standardized in different countries by the migration of capital, and surplus value rates are not standardized by lower labor migration, the organic composition of capital will be also different in those countries.

Another important conclusion is that a developed country cannot extract surplus value from another less developed only through trade, since, as we have seen, surplus value is a magnitude associated with production activities. Any gain arising in international trade will come from a surplus value made in the country of origin, where the good was produced. To extract surplus value of an underdeveloped country, foreign capital should settle on it and produce commodities and surplus value in the host country.

A generalized interpretation of Marxist authors is that the characteristics of the world economy, both as regards trade as to capital movements, tend to delay the problems associated with the contradictions produced by the accumulation of capital, in particular the propensity to crises due to the overproduction or under consumption; as we have already discussed these crises in previous chapters, that analysis will not be repeated.

Another distinctive factor of the world economy is the increased susceptibility of Governments to take decidedly a stand between conflicting interests abroad obviously to support that of nationals. This is possible since they manage to obtain backing of the society unified after a real or alleged "national interest" uniting different classes and sectors behind the policy of the Government, appealing if it is necessary to nationalism and chauvinism. This support is much more difficult to obtain in issues of domestic economy, where the various sectors have clearly conflicting interests. According to some Marxist authors, in a country's international economic relations tend to predominate the interests of capitalists and their associated classes, such as landowners, since it is their products that must be protected against competition from imported products, or on the contrary help to sell them outside. The working class, whose commodity is the labor force that is not tradable internationally, according to these authors, has little at stake in the global economy. This appreciation is when less dubious, given by promoting the export of commodities abroad or hinder the entry of imported commodities, the demand of labor force is actually expanded or protected, thus making the claims of increases in salaries possible and keeping the jobs safe. This is another case in which the inappropriate use of abstraction prevents clearly to make out all of the interests at stake. In reality, there is a community of interests of different classes in the sense of expanding the market for own products; not in all cases prevails a zero-sum game, where what one wins another loses it. There are processes in which all classes and sectors can gain or lose at the same time, and international trade is certainly an arena where such processes take place.

Free trade vs. Protectionism

It is this one of the most important choices in the field of international economic relations. The comparative precedents of greater significance that have been commonly studied are cases of England and United States since the end of the 18th century until the decade of 1870

In England there was a rural noble class with considerable political power and a tradition of strong defense of their interests. Those interests consisted in protecting local food production against cheaper imports from abroad through taxes and other barriers. This originated higher cost of living for the English population and particularly for the working class, and therefore higher values of the variable capital.

The interests of the growing English industry were exactly the opposite. The country industry had an early development, was at the tip of the technology of the time and had economies of scale that other countries could not match. In short it was extremely competitive in quality and price and was not afraid of imported competition. For this reason they developed an ideology of free-market nature, which was the most appropriate for opening markets abroad. One of the most important demands of the industrial sector was the elimination of restrictions on the import of food, which are salary-goods, i.e. goods of which depend the cost of living in particular of the working class and have a strong influence in setting the salary level. The Marxist interpretation points out that this allows raising the rate of surplus value of industrialists by having a lower variable capital.

After years of bitter political fights in England, the burgeoning industrialist class imposed their interests in particular by the abrogation in 1846 of the Corn Laws which turned prohibitive to import grains. This resulted in the political eclipse of nobles, and the country thus became the champion of free trade in the world.

In United States the situation was virtually symmetrical. There was an old landowner class in the southern States, linked to the agricultural production of food and especially cotton, which was the main export product -mainly to England--and for which they required the opening of foreign markets. This made them objectively allies of the English industrial class.

On the other hand, the emerging industry in the northeast states struggled against the imported competition- once more mainly from England- and demanded protection for their products. This objective contradiction between the specific interests of the dominant strata in the southern states and those of the north was, along with the slavery issue and others, one of the causes of the civil war in that country.

Also is this case the civil war ended with the triumph of the industrialist's interests, which, unlike the English, were protectionist. However this was not a protectionist ideology at all costs but that it was justified as necessary in the period that American industry needed to develop and match the competitive advantages of the English. In the background the liberal ideology was underlying as the most appropriate global paradigm, and once the United States managed to become a global industrial power, they tacked on its strategy to the defense of free trade.

The controversy free trade vs. protectionism has been present in almost all countries and in some measure persists to the present day. In general the development of the events has been a slow evolution from the *mercantilism* of the 18th century to the relatively wide free trade of our days.

The interpretation given above on this subject is not exclusive of the Marxist authors, but that, as we have explained in previous cases, is shared by economists of all trends who try to carry out an objective reading of reality.

Evolution of trade

The mercantilist system lasted until the end of the nineteenth century, establishing severe restrictions on trade between leading countries and their spheres of influence, mainly their colonies. Indeed, Spain, Portugal, Holland, France and England set rigid controls over their colonial empires in such a way to keep for their nationals and companies the benefits of imports of raw materials and export of manufactures, in both cases on an exclusive basis: in general the exchange with third countries was forbidden, although smuggling was very difficult to avoid. For example, the port of the city of Buenos Aires, on the principles little more than a village, was an active center of contraband, given its character of marginal and remote, away from all the main routes by their distance from Lima that turned it hard to control by Spain.

This mercantilist system relaxed gradually, not to a lesser extent by the independence processes of the territories of North and South America and finally received a coup de grace at the hands of the English industry, reluctant to any restriction to its unlimited expansion. Although the expansion of colonial empires continued until the end of the 19th century, the area of mercantilism was reduced spatially, as said in a progressive way.

With the advent of the monopoly stage of capitalism-Marxist analysis continues- a new phenomenon comes to light. We saw before that the companies that enjoy monopoly privileges in their markets of origin tend to limit production because in that way they keep the monopolistic extra-profits, which would diminish if the market were supplied in excess. This however produces profits by keeping production facilities partially dormant. Accessing global markets allows the central powers to fill that idle capacity, and allows them to access external markets, if necessary, by lowering selling prices to levels that other competitors could hardly match. In this process, called *dumping*, monopolistic firms subsidize their outside sales with the extra monopolistic profits in their domestic markets, managing to optimize its global economy by fully using their production capacity.

These maneuvers have given rise to anti-dumping laws in several countries seeking to limit these predatory practices in their own markets, but these laws are not always easy to apply by lack of information on costs and prices abroad, and the possibility of retaliation of the affected countries.

In the context of the monopolistic fights, continues the Marxist analysis, the fight between a small group of European powers by the conquest of colonies around the world is exacerbated. In Africa, which until the mid-19th century only had some - but important – Europeans enclaves, was completely colonized by England France, Belgium, and to a lesser extent Germany and Portugal. The colonies were also expanded in different parts of Asia. The reasons were strongly linked to economic issues, both with regard to reserves of domestic markets in areas conquered for the dominant power companies as well as to ensure supplies of raw material supplied by the colonies.

In that period important exports of capital took place directed to the new colonies as well as to independent countries in America; such investments were generally oriented to farming and mining- to provide raw material to the metropolis- railways, port and communication facilities to extract these products and carry them to Europe, other works of infrastructure works with the same object, and commercial activities. Investments in industries that could compete with the metropolises were obviously not made.

Marxism devoted many efforts to analyze this process, called imperialism by Lenin, in which a handful of countries came to dominate vast areas of the planet. The world has changed so much since then that these studies have mainly historical value, and although they can certainly explain the genesis of many current situations, its effects have been diluted quickly in the decades after the World War II.

CHAPTER 15

The reformist way

Marxists were not the only ones who have tried to introduce changes in the capitalist system throughout the last couple of centuries, with the aim of humanizing social relations and spread the benefits of the expansion that undoubtedly the system produces to more vast sectors of the population.

Indeed, parties and organizations of liberal or social democratic inspiration have fought for reforms in the system using the political and peaceful way, and discarding the actions of revolutionary type due to the cost in human suffering and limitations on the freedoms that they invariably imply.

We will then make a brief review of the attitude of Marxists with respect to such attempts, which will serve as a prelude to the next chapter, in which the subject of the construction of socialism will be discussed.

The general attitude has been to devalue all reformist efforts, based on the following scheme of ideas:

• To be able to introduce substantive changes in society, the socialist forces must control all the important power spaces, in the political and social levels. This includes Justice, to prevent it from becoming a bourgeois stronghold that manages to neutralize the political reforms.

• They must evict the bourgeoisie of all economic power niches, to avoid that they can sabotage the reform efforts. This is due to the undeniable links between the economic and political levels.

• They must exercise the monopoly of force and violence to prevent that armed actions in defense of the old order abort the process of change. This involves submitting the armed and security forces to the "popular control".

• Sectors of the bourgeoisie will not accept such modifications that would doom them to impotence, so the reformist path is illusory and unworkable.

• The only valid alternative for agents of transformation is to lead a real dictatorship since the beginning, whether it is called unambiguously "dictatorship of the proletariat" or with any alternative fancy name as "popular democracy" or similar. Socialists must not allow the forces of reaction divert, bribe or deter the revolutionaries of their purpose. In these circumstances, allow opposition voices to tell is a luxury they cannot afford.

These are ultimately *maximalist* positions i.e. that assign no value to processes that do not have as unique and necessary corollary the plain and simple establishment of communism at its end. Since masses do not claim this end as the only valid alternative and struggle instead to carry out other processes of reforms that improve their condition gradually but within the capitalist system, it is necessary that "enlightened avant-gardes", i.e. illuminated elites who are aware of the futility of any other course of action address the processes of change on behalf of these masses. It is unnecessary that such avant-gardes consult the masses since their sole interlocutor is History, of which they are exclusive interpreters and to which they are responsible. It is not the first case in which an ideology leads to arrogance and haughtiness.

Needless to say that these points are not always stated explicitly, but there is no need to scratch far beneath the surface to expose them.

The position based on those principles has undergone deep erosion under the merciless action of time and reality, not only in the many countries that have abandoned the socialist orbit, but also in the few ones that still are nominal communists or "people's republics". We read in the Constitution of the People's Republic of China:

"Article 11. The individual economy of urban and rural working people, operated within the limits prescribed by law, is a complement to the socialist public economy. The state protects the lawful rights and interests of the individual economy. The state guides, and helps monitor the individual economy by exercising administrative control".

At the same time, article 13 of the same document states:

" Article 13. The state protects the right of citizens to own lawfully earned income, savings, houses and other lawful property. The state protects by law the right of citizens to inherit private property".

These texts, as suggested by the number of articles, are not marginal but are in the central plexus of the Chinese Constitution, mixed with others that describe the status of the "sacred" public property. The most significant is that they do not describe a transitional state of affairs in a process towards total collectivization of property, but conversely, they come from a country that rises from the darkness of Mao's Cultural Revolution towards a state of prosperity and well-being never known by the population Chinese in its millenary history.

The message is clear: uncompromising collectivism was and is maintained by anachronistic dictatorships that end up squashed (thankfully without bloodshed) or by lyrical theorists who never had the responsibility to govern or interpret the desires of its citizens. Eventually, and despite the jokes of Marx and Lenin that them were pejoratively called "utopian Socialists" or romantic, the reformist path has survived to Marxist orthodoxy.

CHAPTER 16

The construction of socialism

Marx made numerous references to the new society that would emerge, these mentions are scattered in his works and publications, but nowhere is a systematic treatment of the expected process for such transit, which has given rise to innumerable speculations and interpretations of the reasons for such absence, since it is not logical that something as relevant as the nature of the world towards which he intends to lead to all the humanity remains in darkness. Possible reasons for such absence are, amongst others, the following:

• The natural difficulty of imagining such transition and the goal to achieve, which was even farther in the time of Marx.

• The impossibility of deducting and describe this journey and that goal in scientific terms, requirement that Marx self- demanded for his theory.

• The belief that ultimately the masses would desperate claim to get out of capitalism, asphyxiated by their position within that system, rather than feeling attracted by the benefits of an alternative system.

• His conviction that anticipating a certain image of the society proposed to Mankind would only would serve to focus the debate on sterile discussions, instead of targeting the task of overcoming capitalism.

Marx divided the future evolution of the system into two distinguishable parts:

A transitional phase of the capitalist system, supposedly in flames, toward socialism, that would presumably take place through the dictatorship of the proletariat

This stage would still have a very strong mark of the system that society was leaving, which would have to be overcome promptly.

II. The stage of full communism.

In the *Communist Manifesto*, Marx lists a series of measures to be taken in order to begin the transit in the first phase.

I. The land expropriation and use of the agricultural income for public purposes. The collectivization of land opposes the concept of land subdivision among the peasants, that was the true demand of the rural workers, solution considered "reactionary". Getting support or at least the neutrality of the huge peasant masses was a critical goal for communists in any country undergoing a revolutionary process, even in those advanced of the time. It was clearly stated that the peasant masses were to improve their living conditions with the change in order to gain them for the cause of the revolution. Another objective was to increase agricultural production and livestock, to provide more food for the population. None of these goals were accomplished in seventy years of communism in the Soviet Union. Peasant masses never supported the Bolshevik revolution, their attitude was one of discouragement and non-cooperation, and the lack of grain crisis and food shortages were a constant throughout that long period. There is no doubt that the land question, as Marx conceived it and his followers carried it out was a permanent failure.

II. Progressive and strong income tax, actually confiscatory. In the first stage of the construction of socialism income inequalities persist, since businesses owners and salary differential for the supervisory staff are still present. While the new society with equal salaries for all unfolds, a strong tax to higher income will tend to equate the after tax income of the different social strata. In practice, after the extensive aforementioned communist period, incomes of the Soviet State officials, executives of State-owned enterprises and leaders of the Communist Party (the so-called *Nomenklatura* altogether) were much higher than those of ordinary citizens. In reality, the equalization of incomes for all workers is an unattainable utopia if to keep running a State is desired. Different people with different capacities and attitudes for labor will always demand different salaries.

III. Abolition of the right to inheritance. In principle, according to Marx, individuals can only possess consumer commodities for their own use. Therefore, nothing should be inheritable. Indeed, while communism had to accept income inequality for the reason cited in point II, the existence of families more affluent than others in a Communist State cannot be justified. This premise was not fulfilled in practice, since the greater well-being of the members of the State bureaucracy stretched to their families. In the previous chapter we have read in the Chinese Constitution that this principle was abandoned.

IV. Confiscation of the property of emigrants and their enemies. This was a temporary measure in times of Revolution, and was aimed not only to conveying funds to the State but to deprive of them to all counter-revolutionary attempts that the enemies of the Bolsheviks could devise.

V. State monopoly of credit, through a publicly owned bank. This is a temporary measure until the time is reached when all the means of production are in the hands of State. While there still is a remnant of private companies, the State monopolizes the credit leading them to asphyxia due to lack of funds to those that are of no interest and forcing the disappearance of a private financial sector. Once all the production and distribution is centrally planned, there is no need of credit, at least for productive purposes.

VI. Monopoly of communications and transport in the hands of the State. The object is to deprive the bourgeoisie of the management of this important sector and put it under the control of the State for social purposes.

VII. Expansion of industrial and agricultural production under central State planning. The original purpose was to expand the range of commodities for the proletariat, beyond what has been achieved in this area by the capitalist system. The absolute failure of "real socialism" in the USSR and its satellites in supplying consumer commodities to their populations was undoubtedly a key factor in the lack of support of these during the fall of the Communist regime

VIII. Equal obligation to work for all; establishment of "industrial armies", especially in agriculture. Elimination of parasitism; not working will not be an available option, except for children and the elderly. Everybody will have to work in order to ensure a livelihood. The call to form "Industrial armies" in agriculture was connected with the need of changing the personality of the workers, to promote labor efficiency, eliminating attitudes that decrease it.

IX. Abolition of the separation between city and countryside, distribution of the population in the territories. Combination between industry and agriculture. It must not be forgotten that Marx considered farmers as "a barbarian class", and spoke of the "rural life idiotism". Farmers should incorporate life, technological and cultural patterns that occur in cities. Marx recognizes that capitalism achieved the conditions of material development for a "higher synthesis" between industry and agriculture, "one of the first conditions for the community life".

x. Free education for all children. Abolition of child labor in its current form, combination of education and industrial production. At the time that this was written education was neither universal nor free. Marx was probably not thinking about leaving the role of educator in the hands of the State, but rather on public entities that should emerge from within the society, and limiting State action to design the content and to control of learning, perhaps through inspectors of schools as existed in the United States. He did not want that the children be confined schools, but split their time between education, productive activities and gymnastics. The objectives of this combination were achieving integrated human beings and of promoting productivity at work. Indeed, socialism was able to significantly expand the benefits of education anywhere it was implemented. However we must recognize that in the capitalist world, at least in the developed countries and even in the ones with recent development, a process of equivalent nature and results, and it can certainly be said that emphasis on education has everywhere been a prerequisite for the concomitant economic development.

The reading of this Decalogue of measures for immediate implementation for the establishment of the phase of transition to socialism suggests some important conclusions.

First, the verification of the failure of socialism in some essential results, among them:

• Resolution of the land question. Communism could neither achieve the adhesion of the peasantry, nor ensure food self-sufficiency for its population.

• Exceeding capitalism in the expansion of the productive base, productivity per worker or innovation. The capitalist accumulation and incentive system ended prevailed over the Communist countries regarding quantitative or qualitative productivity.

• The expansion of communism to the rest of the world from the original nuclei.

Secondly, the perusal of the mentioned Decalogue clearly depicts the overall image of an all-powerful State, invading all spheres of action of the individual and determining all his actions, subverting its initiative and reducing him to little more than a robot, a worker bee in a vast human beehive. The testimonies of the people who lived behind the iron curtain check that this image properly reflects what was happening in that gray universe.

Dictatorship of the proletariat

After the bloody tyrannies of the Nazi, fascist and Stalinist periods, the disciples of Marx tried to stay away from the connotations of the term dictatorship, arguing that it was actually inspired by the title of dictator used in transitory way in the Roman Republic period, while enemies and external dangers lurked. This would remove from the term the meaning of systematic violation of human rights, unsustainable today.

Such attempts of justification are not consistent. Marx associated the period of dictatorship of the proletariat with a prolonged period of permanent revolution while hard transit from fully capitalist society to full Communist society was taking place. In this phase coexist the revolutionary proletariat with the remaining classes that will try to maintain the status quo. Therefore, Marx did not hesitate to propitiate the removal or transformation of these other classes with violent methods if necessary, although in principle it was recommended to apply economic measures, such as seizures. He explicitly accepted the use of violence for those purposes ("the midwife of history" in his words).

He took as an example of such a dictatorship to the commune of Paris, in which all the authorities were overthrown and replaced by a body with both executive as legislative responsibilities, whose members had immediately revocable powers and in which the army and the police were disbanded and replaced by the citizens in weapons. There is no doubt that Marx assumed that the revolutionary phase would be bountiful in violent episodes, although naturally he blamed them who were defending their situation. It cannot be seriously sustained that Stalinism was a monstrous distortion of Marxism, but only a probable derivation of a process in which Communism triumphed in one country.

Economic transformations:

Marx gave very few details about the system envisaged in the economic sphere in the socialist society during the period of the dictatorship of the proletariat. The following are some clues about specific issues:

• Improvement of the working conditions. It must be remembered the inhuman conditions in which workers in the vast majority of the factories of the nineteenth century worked. To put an end to this injustice was obviously the first priority not only for humanitarian but also political reasons to clearly show that there was am sudden improvement due to the revolution.

• Reduction of the working day. The average duration of the working day was 12 hours. Marx aimed to cut it in half, which had put to work to numerous persons who were not active or were involved in "parasitic" activities. Thus neither the amount of total hours worked not the output would be affected. This measure would put at the disposal of the workers six hours a day, which he called "true wealth"

• Central planning. Its objective is the satisfaction of social needs. So planners, who play a central role in this scheme must obtain a true balance between those properly prioritized needs and human resources, equipment, materials, etc. available. In other words, the usual role of all planning extended to a whole society.

• Workers will receive from society - after certain deductions - exactly what they have given to it. The one who has given more will receive more. They will receive certain certificates that will allow them to withdraw consumption goods from social inventories, in direct proportion to the hours worked. These certificates will replace the money.

• Only consumption goods will go on sale. The means of production and the 'social' media consumption (trains, non-productive lands etc.) will be public.

• It is obvious that Marx assumed that administrators and planners would act with absolute selflessness and honesty, without letting their own interests to influence their decisions. To achieve this he counts on the "class consciousness", which would overcome all human weakness. Similarly, workers would provide planners and managers honest information, not biased by their own interests. The lack of class consciousness of the workers in the vindication of their rights was something that trouble the Socialists of the time.

Real socialism

This book is not site to make a historical narrative about the evolution of communism in those countries where it ruled. It would exceed the length of the book, its purpose focused on the political economy of Marx, and the author´s knowledge. We will restrict to deal with a couple of issues that somehow relate to strategic choices that the leaders of those countries have done.

The expectation of Marx and his immediate followers was that socialism would be imposed by the desperation of the masses starved by capitalism, and that this process would take place more or less simultaneously in the major developed nations, particularly in Germany and the rest of central Europe.

None of these assumptions turned out to be valid. Communism was imposed as late as 1917 in Russia, a backward country, notable more for its rural masses than by its proletariat, that went into crisis with its regime closer to feudalism than to capitalism as a result inter alia of the disastrous impact of the World War I. Communism expanded rapidly through Eastern Europe and China in the aftermath of World War II in devastated countries and in many cases occupied by the Red Army. Its subsequent expansion in Southeast Asia took place after wars of nationalist liberation against colonial and corrupt regimes. In no case a Socialist experience happened as expected as a specifically ant-bourgeois revolution led by a working-class.

Communism took control of an isolated Russia, and once it became evident that it would not spread quickly to the rest of Europe, a controversy known as "socialism in one country" vs. "permanent revolution "was generated inside the socialism. This political dispute was carried out by two opposite sides in the USSR, visibly identified in persons José Stalin and León Trotsky respectively.

Stalinism defended the thesis of carry out the Socialist Revolution in a single country- even in an underdeveloped country like Russia- was a feasible task, that communism could gain a foothold there and constitute a safe rearguard from which to expand the system to the rest of the world where objective conditions made it possible. The Trotskyites argued that that process would be unsustainable in the long run and that the immediate struggle for the worldwide expansion of communism was the only viable route. In the 14th Congress of the Russian Communist Party in 1923 the controversy was settled in favor of Stalin and Trotsky was murdered years later in Mexico.

It is instructive to read the justifications of Stalin on the strategy of socialism in one country. He wrote - and no doubt believed - that capitalism could not long withstand the confrontation with the Soviet Union, and that the masses would turn to socialism because of the higher standard of living that this system would provide them. "Imperialism", namely the capitalist system led to a certain degree of historical development, would disintegrate due to the gravitational attraction of communism. Many people, Marxist or not, shared this belief until the 1960s. What actually subsequently happened, that is the disintegration of the Socialist bloc in the confrontation with capitalism with the acquiescence of the masses in both blocs, was not even an acceptable work hypothesis.

CHAPTER 17

Historical materialism

We begin this chapter with two clarifications about it.

The first relates to its location within the book. Historical materialism is the philosophical and conceptual framework of Marxism, so in an academic work a chapter on this subject would likely be located at the beginning. The author hesitated before locating it near the end of the writing and finally opted to place it immediately before the next (and final) chapter, which somehow a summary of the contents of the book will be made. In this way, the reader (even those making their first weapons in the subject of Marxist political economy) will have fresh its content on this crucial issue.

The second clarification refers to textual quotations from Marx and Engels. In the previous chapters they were reduced to a minimum on the grounds that the references of these authors are often scattered in all their vast work, and not always in a plain, agile and enjoyable language for the common reader of the XXI century. In the case of historical materialism, the quotes we have selected and reproduced - classical quotes in this issue - are of an unparalleled expositional clarity and a conceptual density, which will not require further explanations. The author considers that he has nothing to add to them.

Sources

In Chapter 3 of his work of Socialism: Utopian and Scientific Friedrich Engels wrote:

"The materialist conception of history starts from the proposition that the production of the means to support human life and, next to production, the exchange of things produced, is the basis of all social structure; that in every society that has appeared in history, the manner in which wealth is distributed and society divided into classes or orders is dependent upon what is produced, how it is produced, and how the products are exchanged. *From this point of view, the final causes of all social changes and political revolutions are to be sought, not in men's brains, not in men's better insights into eternal truth and justice, but in changes in the modes of production and exchange. They are to be sought, not in the* philosophy, *but in the* economics *of each particular epoch.* The growing perception that existing social institutions are unreasonable and unjust, that reason has become unreason, and right wrong [1], is only proof that in the modes of production and exchange changes have silently taken place with which the social order, adapted to earlier economic conditions, is no longer in keeping. From this it also follows that the means of getting rid of the incongruities that have been brought to light must also be present, in a more or less developed condition, within the changed modes of production themselves. These means are not to be invented by deduction from fundamental principles, but are to be discovered in the stubborn facts of the existing system of production".

Later and referred to capitalism Engels adds:

"The present situation of society — this is now pretty generally conceded — is the creation of the ruling class of today, of the bourgeoisie. The mode of production peculiar to the bourgeoisie, known, since Marx, as the capitalist mode of production, was incompatible with the feudal system, with the privileges it conferred upon individuals, entire social ranks and local corporations, as well as with the hereditary ties of subordination which constituted the framework of its social organization. The bourgeoisie broke up the feudal system and built upon its ruins the capitalist order of society, the kingdom of free competition, of personal liberty, of the equality, before the law, of all commodity owners, of all the rest of the capitalist blessings. Thenceforward, the capitalist mode of production could develop in freedom. Since steam, machinery, and the making of machines by machinery transformed the older manufacture into modern industry, the productive forces, evolved under the guidance of the bourgeoisie, developed with rapidity and in a degree unheard of before. But just as the older manufacture, in its time, and handicraft, becoming more developed under its influence, had come into collision with the feudal trammels of the guilds, so now modern industry, in its complete development, comes into collision with the bounds within which the capitalist mode of production holds it confined. The new productive forces have already outgrown the capitalistic mode of using them. And this conflict between productive forces and modes of production is not a conflict engendered in the mind of man, like that between original sin and divine justice. It exists, in fact, objectively, outside us, independently of the will and actions even of the men that have brought it on. Modern Socialism is nothing but the reflex, in thought, of this conflict in fact; its ideal reflection in the minds, first, of the class directly suffering under it, the working class."

You don't need to add anything to clarify the meaning of these extensive paragraphs; we will only emphasize the sequence of ideas that are expressed here:

• The foundation of all social order lies in the modes of production and exchange of commodities.

• Production and exchange depend on the division of humans into social classes, and the distribution of commodities associated with this class divide.

• Social and political changes have their origin in the transformations in those modes of production, and not abstract ideas that emerge in the heads of men by spontaneous generation.

• The perception that existing social institutions are unfair comes from the mismatch between those institutions and the new conditions of production and exchange.

• When this perception is imposed on society, it is a clear sign that the germs of new relations of production and change already existing in the society.

Meanwhile Marx writes in his Preface of *A Contribution to the Critique of Political Economy*

"In the social production of their life, men enter into definite relations that are indispensable and independent of their will, relations of production which correspond to a definite stage of development of their material productive forces. The sum total of these relations of production constitutes the economic structure of society, the real foundation, on which rises a legal and political superstructure and to which correspond definite forms of social consciousness.

The mode of production of material life conditions the social, political and intellectual life process in general. It is not the consciousness of men that determines their being, but, on the contrary, their social being that determines their consciousness.

At a certain stage of their development, the material productive forces of society come in conflict with the existing relations of production, or — what is but a legal expression for the same thing — with the property relations within which they have been at work hitherto. From forms of development of the productive forces these relations turn into their fetters.

Then begins an epoch of social revolution. With the change of the economic foundation the entire immense superstructure is more or less rapidly transformed. In considering such transformations a distinction should always be made between the material transformation of the economic conditions of production, which can be determined with the precision of natural science, and the legal, political, religious, aesthetic or philosophic — in short, ideological forms in which men become conscious of this conflict and fight it out. Just as our opinion of an individual is not based on what he thinks of himself, so we cannot judge of such a period of transformation by its own consciousness; on the contrary, this consciousness must be explained rather from the contradictions of material life, from the existing conflict between the social productive forces and the relations of production.

No social order ever perishes before all the productive forces for which there is room in it have developed; and new, higher relations of production never appear before the material conditions of their existence have matured in the womb of the old society itself. Therefore mankind always sets itself only such tasks as it can solve; since, looking at the matter more closely, it will always be found that the tasks itself arises only when the material conditions of its solution already exist or are at least in the process of formation."

Although completely coincident with the previous paragraph of Engels in its content, the text of Marx has its own expressiveness, so we consider convenient to include it. Once again and slightly altering the order in which the ideas appear, we can discern the following core concepts:

• In their social life men established relations of production independent of their will.

• The nature of these relationships depends on the degree of development of the productive forces at that time and that place. Within the relations of production the property relations occupy a central role.

• The set of production and exchange relationships form the economic structure of society. This structure raises the legal and political superstructure.

• Values ("forms of social consciousness") underpinning this superstructure is not dependent of the free evolution of the human spirit, but in the material conditions of life.

• There Marx introduced his famous phrase... "The anatomy of civil society must be sought in the political economy".

• Before a social formation disappears and new relations of production come into force their conditions must have matured in the ancient society.

• Therefore, no society proposes itself objectives it is unable to reach. ....

As we can see, in both exposure of Engels and Marx, there is a hard core of very coherent and integrated concepts. It is on this theoretical basis that historical materialism is built.

Criticism of the materialistic interpretation of history

Historical materialism so defined by Marx has been great progress in the analysis of the causes and the development of the socio-economic systems, tearing the ideological veils that had covered them up to then, but ended up creating an economicist determinism, that the same Engels came to glimpse and report once dead Marx. One thing is to introduce the material bases that explain social phenomena, particularly those of change, and another is to deny the involvement of any other causal, attributing it to a vague "general evolution of the human spirit". Linking every variation in the paradigms of an era to a change in property relations is a gross oversimplification that leaves an infinite number of aspects without explaining, such as the different impact on different societies of a same change in relations of production.

Additionally, the reduction of the more general term "relations of production" to the mere concept of ownership relationships impoverishes the analysis leaving in the dark aspects that are important in the material development of the productive forces of different cultures and societies, such as the relative availability of raw material, energy sources, trade routes, craft traditions, agrarian and industrial technologies, general cultural level, etc. The last mentioned for example, is an aspect associated with super structural levels, and has however a huge and growing importance in the productive development of a society, which shows that the superstructure is not only a passive receiver of economic influences, but structure and superstructure are not watertight compartments and there is a dynamic interaction between their components.

What happens is that in the time of Marx and Engels was in force in the physical sciences a mechanistic paradigm that was believed to be able to explain the universe by the interaction of simple forces on simple bodies. Today, under the influence of quantum theory and Heisenberg's uncertainty principle, all the old certainties have fallen, and it is expedient to go to more uncertain and complex explanations. On the other hand, the human mind is not considered today a simple *tabula rasa* where external economic and social events simply print their effects, but that we know that it is an autonomous and enigmatic and at once wonderful and scary organ.

In short, recognizing the validity of the base of historical materialism, it is necessary to make a more nuanced interpretation of its effects, admitting developments coming from the interior of the human being, although it is true that they require at times certain external conditions to come to light.

CHAPTER 18

The legacy

To make a balance with pretensions of definitive of Marxist political economy greatly exceeds the possibilities of this author and this book. However, in the preceding pages some general guidelines on the subject have been exposed, and it is possible to advance some interim conclusions, in order to stimulate further discussion. If he succeeds in making a contribution to such serious and respectful debate, the author's purpose regarding this project would be fulfilled

Marx created the materialistic interpretation of history not as an aseptic and impartial tool of social inquiry, but as a blunt weapon that served him in the lid to overthrow bourgeois society and implement communism in its place. The fall of capitalism by the weight of its internal contradictions and the inevitability of the socialist road were not ex post conclusions to which Marx arrived after a cold and dispassionate analysis, but his *a priori* thesis, his selected destination port, based on which he guided his conceptual boat rudder, selecting the levels of abstraction that he applied; i.e. the elements of reality chosen for analysis and those ignored, arguments and evidence which he elected on the basis of whether they pointed towards the desired goal. The conclusions relied on these chosen arguments, and when there were factors limiting the scope of such arguments, he silenced them in waiting that the future would prove that abstraction selected was correct and the discarded elements were simple ephemeral details.

We cannot call into question the intellectual honesty of Marx, deeply convinced of his points of view, and must recognize that believed he was moving in what he perceived as the clear direction indicated by History. It is difficult to conceive that he could foresee the fate of communist society after seven decades of rule.

It would not be correct to blame the leadership of the countries of the Soviet orbit for having deviously betrayed the teachings of the master. In fact, this is the attitude of many current Marxists, who only try to separate Marx from two extremely unfortunate facts:

• The history of tyranny, repression, deprivation of individual liberties and trampling of human rights in the communist countries, which the communist leadership supported at the time, but today, would be unjustifiable.

• Evidence of the collapse of the Communist system in all over the world.

In reality, and referring to its Marxist variant, we must soberly consider that the so-called "real socialism" was indeed the possible socialism, at least in Marxist version. There is an undeniable thin red thread that leads from the concepts of "dictatorship of the proletariat" and "violence as a midwife of History" to the Gulags, "neuropsychiatric institutes" in Siberia, Mao´s Cultural Revolution and the extermination camps of Pol Pot. There is no way to take charge of Marxist theory and not of its consequences. Otherwise, capitalism could deny its involvement in the colonial wars and the formation of

Empires, and even supporters of the Aryan superiority theory might argue they have nothing to do with Hitler's "excesses" or betrayal.

Those who seriously claim to be the heirs to the legacy of Kart Marx character must accept that it was a powerful and original intellect but also was a product of his time, a merciless time. In an effort of abstraction - that his master would surely approve - they must determine what has been the real contribution that the thinker made to economic and social analysis and throw overboard what failed and rescue and re-contextualize those teachings that have withstood the passage of time.

The classical repertoire of guides to political action based on the class struggle, the recurrence to violence as an engine of the story, the action of enlightened elites and the establishment of the dictatorship of the proletariat has been a dead-end road and even more, they are unrepeatable today for they are not in the current *zeitgeist*, the spirit of the current era.

The author considers that the lasting contribution lies mainly in the analysis methodology of Marx, based on historical materialism with the limitations suggested in the previous chapter. This methodology, applied with an open mind to the study of the current situation and future prospects, untethered to fixed conclusions obtained a century and a half ago, should give new fruits.

BIBLIOGRAPHY

Karl Marx

1. Capital. A critique of political economy; Volume I-Penguin Classics. 1976
2. Capital-Volume II-Marx Engels Internet Archive. Marx- Engels Library-2007
3. Capital. Volume III-The process of capitalist production as a whole-Marx Engels Internet Archive. Marx- Engels Library-2010
4. Wage-labor and capital-Marx Engels Internet Archive. Marx- Engels Library-2006
5. A critique of the Botha program-Marx Engels Internet Archive. Marx- Engels Library—1999
6. A preface to a contribution to the critique of political economy-Marx Engels Internet Archive. Marx- Engels Library-2002
7. A Contribution to the Critique of Political Economy-Marx Engels Internet Archive. Marx-Engels Library-2009
8. The eighteenth Brumaire of Louis Bonaparte-Marx Engels Internet Archive. Marx- Engels Library-2010
9. The civil war in France-Marx Engels Internet Archive. Marx- Engels Library-2009
10. The poverty of philosophy-Marx Engels Internet Archive. Marx- Engels Library-2006

11. **Karl Marx and Friedrich Engels**

12. A critique of German ideology-Marx Engels
Internet Archive. Marx- Engels Library-2000
13. The Communist Manifesto-Marx Engels
Internet Archive. Marx- Engels Library-2000

14. **Friedrich Engels**
15. Socialism: Utopian and Scientific-Marx Engels
Internet Archive. Marx- Engels Library-2003
16. The principles of Communism-Marx Engels
Internet Archive. Marx- Engels Library-2005

17. **Paul M. Sweezy**
18. The Theory of Capitalist Development.
Principles of Marxian Political Economy-
Monthly Review Press.

WORKS BY OSCAR RIGIROLI

FICTION

Distant ice

Golden legend

Ordo Australis

South of Capricorn

CRITICAL ESSAY

The political economy of Marx

COORDINATES OF THE AUTHOR

Personal blog:
http://narrativaoscarrigiroli.wordpress.com/

Twitter:@OscarRigiroli

origiroli@gmail.com